THE SENSUOUS COUPLE

The
Sensuous Couple

by

Dr. 'C'

NEW ENGLISH LIBRARY
TIMES MIRROR

An NEL Original

© 1971 by Dr. 'C'

*

FIRST NEL EDITION SEPTEMBER 1971

*

NEL Books are published by New English Library Limited from Barnard's Inn, Holborn, London, EC1. Made and printed in Great Britain by Love & Malcomson Ltd., Redhill, Surrey.

450010732

CONTENTS

CHAPTER ONE

SENSUOUS WOMAN, SENSUOUS MAN—SO WHAT NOW?

So, you are a Sensuous Woman!

So, you are a Sensuous Man!

Solitary sex isn't all that fun, though it's better than nothing; so to put all the knowledge you've gained to good account, you've got to be sensuous, not only to, but *with*, one another. In other words, you've got to become a Sensuous Couple.

And don't make the mistake that so many couples do, of imagining that because they've learned to be sensuous in a number of ways, what turns one on turns all on. Not only that, Pelvis Thrusts and Vaginal Contractions may make a man wild one day, but merely irritate him the next.

Every love session has to be played by ear. This doesn't only go for the first time casual encounter; it goes for every session in a long and regular relationship.

Nothing upsets the responses to sex so much as both partners taking one another for granted. You may have a satisfactory climax sensationwise and feel satisfied when it's over, but if you've made love mechanically—and the most Sensuous Man and the most Sensuous Woman can fall into that trap—you won't have that strangely paradoxical sensation of exhilarated contentment that is the real reward of a thoughtful—not thought-out—planned session.

From one moment to the next you should not know what you are going to do to your partner, nor he/she to you.

This means that the Sensuous Man and the Sensuous Woman have got to be quick thinkers and quick reactors who never miss a trick, if they want to become a Sensuous Couple.

You can't make thrilling love, however sensuous you are, unless you know him and he knows you so well that there is not a single square millimetre of each of your bodies that you haven't caressed with every type of caress you know—and if you're sensuous you know the lot—have seen how it reacts and stored the information away for future reference at the half-flicker of an eyelid.

You took a lot of trouble making yourself sensuous; now you've got to take even more to make your partner respond sensuously to you.

I'm going on rather about all this, but I'm sure it is the most important aspect of making love. Couples just don't take the trouble to get to know one another's bodies and their responses thoroughly, and one of the reasons why they don't is because they don't give enough time to their lovemaking.

The quick stand-up job behind the bushes on the golf course relieves a throbbing erection of penis or clitoris and it may remain in the memory because of the setting and the circumstances and the excitement or the risk of being seen, but it's only the kind of sex that momentarily satisfies, and it's 90 per cent physical, 10 per cent cerebral, whereas a good session should be 100 per cent physical, 100 per cent cerebral. And, if that seems madly illogical, and impossible, it is not! The physical and the cerebral should, in fact, *must* coincide; if they do—and they can be made to— the results will defy description even by a Shakespeare.

What are you aiming for when you make love?

You've gone to the trouble of making yourselves into Sensuous Men and Sensuous Women, so obviously you are aiming for physical response.

In my experience this is not enough. Certainly, sex should be fun, full of laughter and happiness. A mistake that many couples make—especially young couples—is to treat it too seriously. On the other hand, though, there has got to be emotional contact.

Ever since I began to talk and write about such things, I've always maintained that with couples who have sex together regularly, whether married or single, the physical sex should be a visible, tangible expression of the emotional love the partners have for one another. I'm sure I'm right about this, because if you use physical sex on this basis, it takes on a significance which no other species can inject into their sex. It gives a meaning to the whole thing which otherwise is lacking, because if you make love only for the physical experience you are downgrading both yourself and your partner to the level of the farmyard.

But it goes even deeper than that. If you make physical love to your partner to express your love for him or her, you must aim always at giving him/her the greatest possible physical experience that you, your partner and various other circumstances can produce. After all, isn't that why you have taken the trouble to transform yourselves into a Sensuous Man, a Sensuous Woman?

The whole point of making love on this basis, however, is that it prevents you from being selfish. One of the commonest and most long-standing complaints of frustrated partners is, "You only want me for your own pleasure!" If you are aiming to give your partner an experience that is truly worthwhile, you forget about yourself and concentrate on the other body. Your partner will take care of yours.

Remember, too, I said that the *couple* make love to express the emotional love *each* has for the other.

So it's just got to be a two-way process. The woman must see that her lover is turned on to distraction just as much as he must see that she is led forward and finally catapulted into a new world, a paradisean world, of human experience.

So it's a partnership, in which both have equal responsibilities towards one another.

Despite what some people may have suggested, you haven't become a Sensuous Woman so that you can attract a man to make love to you; and you haven't become a Sensuous Man so that every woman who knows your reputation or who recognises your opening gambits will fall flat on her back at the sight of you. You have become a Sensuous Couple so that when you do eventually join up physically you become truly the Two-Backed Beast, the plural become singular, in complete and total mental-physical fusion.

And if you think that doing it this way means that you can't have fun, don't you believe it!

When you really know one another and are convinced of your mutual love, you don't have to keep reminding yourself of it. The serious intention will always be there if you devote yourselves to each other's pleasuring, make no mistake about that!

So let your love-sex be fun-sex. I don't mind bet-

ting that it is the love-sex that will finally hit you between the eyes in those magnificent post-orgasm
moments, when you've come back to an unrecognis-
ably comfortable world, and you are grateful for what
your partner has done for you.

That's when you'll think of love, of what you've
been able to share, and your happiness and your satisfaction will be all the greater if it's been achieved in
light-hearted gaiety and laughter.

The thunder in your ears as you climaxed will be
heard now as the distant crashing chords of a mighty
organ; and the sweat that is irradiating your now love-
replete bodies is the divine unction with which you
were anointed for your sacred dances in the Temple
of Love.

In my book, the slam-bam is out, except on certain
rare occasions when *both* partners are so high on sex
before the clothes come off; when it would serve no
purpose to wait and would, in fact, be a crime against
nature to wait, since two bodies and spirits so attuned
can only be in both sorts, lovers in love. For me, the
slam-bam, as Dr Reuben put it in another context, is
merely vaginal masturbation for both, unless it happens as I've just described, and I can see no point in
it except the glans penis, and perhaps—only perhaps
—the clitoral tip. You can get the same effect with a
good lubricant and one's own fingers, and it seems a
shocking waste of material, effort and even the few
minutes it takes.

But I realise I am preaching to the converted. The
truly Sensuous Man and the truly Sensuous Woman
know that love-fun sex must have certain pre-condi-
tions if it is to be successful—of milieu, time and communication.

CHAPTER TWO

THE SETTING

"I am dead against the back-seat of a car; dead against the sweet-scented springy bed of a pine forest; dead against lush grass in an intimate field."

That was me speaking to eight hundred students at Aston University last October, on *How to Enjoy Sex*.

I went on, "Because of the acrobatics involved, I've never yet met a woman who has climaxed in the back seat of a car by penis-vagina contact, nor a man who has achieved anything but too rapid ejaculation, if he reaches that point at all. Pine needles are extraordinarily abrasive in the wrong places at any time and definitely anti-orgasm at certain times; while the unseen insect life in the lush grass of a hay-field makes itself felt unfailingly at the most crucial moments."

What I was trying to impress on my audience was that for successful lovemaking, a degree of comfort—among several other things—is a first essential.

THE BEDROOM

Though the Sensuous Man and the Sensuous Woman have learned that anywhere in the house is a potential lovemaking scene, the fact is that even Sensuous Couples have most of their encounters in bed, while Unsensuous Couples invariably do.

This being so, care should be given to the choice of bedroom and to its furnishing and equipment.

Ideally, the room should be sound-proof. I don't mean that a vast amount of money should be spent on elaborate sound-proofing gadgetry, but it should be a room where the sounds that lovers may make are not heard in other parts of the house or apartment, or in adjoining apartments or houses.

In advising this, I know I am advising the impossible in a very large number of cases, but I am convinced of the value of lovemaking sounds as a sexually arousing factor, that I urge careful thought to be given to this point. (I'll be saying more about lovemaking sounds later.)

Nothing can be more restraining, or indeed off-putting, than for a couple to be conscious of the fact that they can be overheard while making love. In fact, many a would-be Sensuous Couple have been prevented from becoming so by the fear that what they say to one another, the moans, whimpers and cries, the ohs-and-ahs of high appreciation, the pantings and the encouragements may reach the ears of others outside the room.

The worst sufferers from this possibility as far as outsiders are concerned, are those who live in modern semi-detached houses or apartment blocks. Mind you, I don't think that one need always worry about being overheard in certain situations, because not only are sounds stimulating to the lovers themselves, they can be equally stimulating to those who overhear them, provided the possible audience are in the same age-group as oneself and are a Sensuous Couple, or have Sensuous Couple potential. In these circumstances is it sporting to deprive anyone of an aid to more splendid arousal? It is certainly stupid to deprive oneself of a free-bonus if the neighbours turn out to be erolalists,* too.

Two couples I know who once lived next to one another in a block of new apartments, discovered this. They had moved into their respective apartments within a few weeks of one another. For Alice and Jim, it was their first home, while Grace and Reg, who had been married two or three years, had formerly lived in the top floor apartment of a solidly built, converted detached Victorian house.

Grace and Reg, well on the way to being a Sensuous Couple, were noisy lovers. Grace had always been so naturally, and when Reg realised what a stimulating technique it was, not only for Grace but himself, he had adopted it. As things got going, they made quite a shindy between them, and because they had had no complaints or sidelong looks from the neighbours on the floor below, it had never entered their heads that others might overhear them vocalising their loving.

Alice and Jim had had sex fairly regularly for a couple of years before they married, and so were no wide-eyed innocents. On the other hand they had not yet become so adeptly sensuous as Grace and Reg,

---

* *Erolalia* (my own invention) means *love-noises*; not to be confused with the psychiatrist's terms *erotolalia* and *coprolalia*, which are defined as "the use of tabooed sexual terms during, or in connection with, intercourse." These two are compulsive rather than deliberate, while my erolalia, referring to noises—though words can be used, but they need not necessarily be four-letter words or other tabooed sexual terms—need not be compulsive, but acquired. If the technique is not compulsive, it should be learned. No Sensuous Couple can afford to be without it. (See Chapter 11.)

though they were no prigs and were eagerly experimental.

Neither couple had any children at this time, and all of them had jobs. Sunday mornings, therefore, were leisure mornings for both couples, and as young couples eager and in love customarily do, they passed the greater part of the morning—and often the afternoon as well, especially if it was wet or cold—between cups of coffee and slices of toast and an orgasm or two—or three.

Alice and Jim had moved in on the Saturday. Grace and Reg, who were tenants of two or three weeks' standing and so were settled down, gave them supper, as much to run an eye over them as to act the Good Samaritans. What they saw and heard they liked, but being townspeople made no final judgment then.

The younger couple were exhausted after a strenuous day of humping furniture, and excused themselves soon after supper. About half-past ten next morning Alice dug Jim sharply in the ribs.

"Listen!" she whispered. When Jim merely grunted, she dug him in the ribs until he was properly awake. "Whatever do you think they're doing?"

Jim listened, as mystified as Alice.

"I don't know," he said truthfully. "He's probably beating her up."

"I thought he had cruel eyes," Alice commented quite unjustifiably. "Do you think we ought to do something about it?"

"Certainly not!" Jim retorted sharply. "It's a cardinal rule of human society never to interfere between husband and wife."

"He must be hurting her."

"Put your head under the bed-clothes and you won't

hear. I'll go and make a cup of tea."

When Jim came back with the tea, all was quiet next door.

"I don't think we ought to get to know them," Alice suggested.

"Last night you were saying how fine it was to have kind neighbours. Anyway, living next door you can't ignore them."

"Well, we can be distant."

It happened again during the week—it happened more than once, but Alice and Jim only heard them once—and again next Sunday morning.

"It's funny," Alice said. "She doesn't look as if he beats her up."

"I'd say they were in love, from the little I've seen of them," Jim suggested.

At that moment a lusty gust of vocalised male delight dominated the higher-pitched female cries.

They had not heard Reg's erolalia before, probably owing to a number of reasons.

"Oh god!" Jim whispered. "That's what they're doing?"

"What?" Alice whispered back.

"Making love! I remember reading somewhere that some people groan, and moan, and cry out."

"I don't think it's quite nice," Alice commented.

"Oh, come off it!" Jim protested. "You know you don't believe that!"

"No, I didn't mean that. I meant, it's not nice to hear them."

"Oh, I don't know," Jim grinned. "Here—feel that! It wasn't there a minute ago."

"You're terrible!" Alice giggled, but didn't take her hand away.

Soon it got so that they waited to hear next-door's erolalia; and being honest, they had to confess that it excited them.

It was Jim who began it. Alice didn't say anything the first time, but he could tell it excited her. Then after a time, she joined him.

When Grace and Reg first heard them, their first reaction was, "They must be able to hear us, too."

"Do you think we ought to apologise?" Grace asked.

"I don't think so, not now they're doing it as well."

But Grace did mention it to Alice, when they were having coffee together one Saturday morning.

"I hope we don't disturb you," she said.

"We never hear you," Alice told her, completely misunderstanding her. "It's a good arrangement having the sitting-rooms on opposite sides of the flat."

"No, I mean in the bedroom," Grace said.

"Oh, that," Alice blushed. "Well, you had us puzzled at first, but when we realised what you were doing, we thought we'd try it out too. We often try and wait until you're making love, because it's so exciting. Have you noticed?"

"Now you mention it." They laughed. "Well, that's all right then. I thought we ought to say something."

"Do you mind about us?"

"Of course not. Reg was saying only yesterday, it's good to have kindred spirits as neighbours."

After that, they never mentioned it, or even hinted at it, all the years that they were neighbours; except on one occasion when Jim told Reg what had happened the first time they had eavesdropped.

Grace and Reg told me that it had added a new dimension to their lovemaking.

Had Alice and Jim been a middle-aged or elderly couple, I would have expected Grace and Reg to do something to make the likelihood of their being overheard less. There are available now various materials that are fairly cheap and easy to fix, which give quite a high degree of sound-proofing. Generally only one wall needs attention. (Ask your Do-It-Yourself shopman's advice.) But the Sensuous Couple are a thoughtful pair, and the last thing they want to do is to obtrude their sex lives so that others are embarrassed.

Of course there are cases in which actual sound-proofing is not feasible. Then the Sensuous Couple will, if they are erolalists, make love against a background of music, not played so loudly that it is disturbing, but loudly enough to smother most of their own sounds; and they will make more frequent use of other rooms for sexual encounters.

Should there be children or elderly people living in the house, if possible their bedrooms should not adjoin the couple's room. Old people are not only embarrassed but can become highly jealous if, deprived of sexual outlets themselves, they are subjected to the erotic goings on of younger folk; while small children can be frightened by what they hear because they do not understand what is happening and older children, who do understand, can be given such a disgust of sex that they never function normally sexually throughout their adult lives. For some strange reason, sexually-knowledgeable adolescents, forgetting how they got into the world, tend not to associate sex with mummy and daddy.

There is the other side of the coin, too. Younger couples can be thrown off balance if they think they can be overheard by children or older people; and nothing puts the guilt more surely on the gingerbread than having to worry about others—either overhearing or interrupting—when one is having sex.

Talking of interruptions, I am old-fashioned enough to think that the parents' bedroom should be their refuge from the rest of the family and from family responsibilities. I don't agree with toddlers being taken into the parents' bed, and even less with four or five year olds creeping in on a Sunday morning's late lie-in.

Some young parents I know, who are honestly trying to raise their families on the highly laudable principle that sex is a natural part of living, all open and above-board, have started taking their babies and one year olds into bed with them sometimes so that the kiddies can see them naked in bed, and grow up to think nothing of it. I am sure that sooner or later they are going to regret it, because sooner or later the five or six year olds will want to join them at times when they want to be on the job; and how are little children to be made to understand that what is convenient once is not always convenient?

Let the bedroom door have a lock or bolt until the child is old enough to be reasoned with and told that mummy and daddy sometimes want to be alone together. This is not to say that children are to be permanently excluded from the bedroom. On the contrary, parents should invite them in from time to time, and the operative word is *invite*—but not allow them in their beds.

A couple I know, who devoted most Sunday afternoons in winter and at holiday times to lovemaking, saw no reason why they should stop their sensuous custom when the children reached puberty and could guess what they were up to. Taking the bull by the horns, they blatantly hung a *Do Not Disturb* notice on the bedroom door at such times, and gave strict instructions that they were not to be disturbed on any account so long as the notice was there, not even for the telephone.

One afternoon the telephone rang and Robert, who was twelve, answered it. An hour or two later an embarrassed but irate grandmother arrived.

"I'm surprised at you two," she fulminated.

"But why?" they asked.

"I rang up because I wanted to speak to Debbie; little Robert answered, and do you know what he said?—'She can't speak to you now because she's making love with Dad.'"

"But he's only twelve, mother-in-law. He didn't mean to be impolite."

"What do you mean—impolite? He was most polite. It was what he said."

"But we were making love, mother!"

"I'm disgusted with you. No—I don't mean that. I'm disgusted that you don't keep it from that dear little boy."

"But he knows all about it, mother!"

(They had overheard him a month or two back telling his younger brother on the landing, "You can't see Mum, because they're making love.")

"You make me despair!" groaned Grannie. "Innocence doesn't seem to count any more."

I am all in favour of parents and children being naked together, so long as the practice is inaugurated at an early age. But in the bathroom and the bath, in the bedroom occasionally and the rest of the house at any time—but not the connubial bed!

By this time I can hear you saying, "But what the hell has all this to do with the Sensuous Couple?"

It has a great deal!

Because parents, sons, daughters, sons-in-law and daughters-in-law have just as much right to be Sensuous Couples as anyone else—even more right.

Right! Your bedroom is sound-proof, if that is necessary; and there is a lock or bolt on the door to keep out fun-spoiling kiddies. It is your play-room—as well as your sanctuary—so what about its furniture and the toys?

The Bed

At the top of the list is the bed.

Not half enough attention is given to the bed in any case; yet we spend at least one-third of our lives in it, and much more if we're a Sensuous Couple. As a rule, the man will defer to the wishes of his partner, and though I hesitate to say it, even the most sex-conscious women are apt to go more for appearances than for practicality, unless they are guided.

Anyone, single or plural, who thinks he can make love on a three-foot-six bed is a fool.

The Sensuous Couple have got to have room for manoeuvre. Two people, not even two males, or two females, can make love satisfactorily on less than thirty square feet of bed. The Sensuous Couple are much more comfortable with more.

Note that I have said *on*.

The Sensuous Couple do not, under any circumstances, make love *in* bed.

They make love *on* the bed.

And when I say on the bed, take care! Making love is a strenuous business. If it isn't, you're not making love, you're just playing around.

Since it is strenuous, you're going to get hot. If you follow my simple advice, and make love on the bed, rather than in it, if you wrestle on a thick blanket, you might just as well be wrestling under it.

So—pull the top covers right back; better, remove them completely; and go to it on the fresh white pasture—or coloured, if you like coloured bed-linen—of the under-sheet.

The bed is vastly important, and must be selected with great thought.

Make it as large as you can without overcrowding the room with it. As I have said, the Sensuous Couple need as much room for manoeuvre as they can get.

Choose the mattress carefully. It needs to be firm, and yet soft enough to sleep on comfortably.

Whatever else it does, it must not rattle or squeak even when it is transformed into a lovers' trampoline.

Supply it well with pillows. Even if you are not going to sleep on all of them, the Sensuous Couple can always find other excellent uses for them.

The Floor

Whatever you do to the rest of the flooring in the house, do let yourself go in the bedroom and have a good quality wall-to-wall carpet fitted. If you are not millionaires, and can't afford one with a two-inch-long pile, go for a quality you can easily afford, and then splash out on a really luxurious foam-rubber underlay—which usually won't cost you more than a third of the price of the carpet. This type of underlay is sensuous-making when the carpet is walked on with bare feet, and comfortable for doing those other things on, which you learned while studying to be a Sensuous

Couple and which are more safely done on a firm base.

Temperature

The temperature of the bedroom is also high on the list of priorities.

You can't make love *on* the bed, or on the floor, or anywhere else in the room, for that matter, with blue tits and brass balls. Though you will undoubtedly warm up after you've been going at it for a time, it's hard even to make a start if your teeth are chattering and you feel as if you've just rolled in the snow.

Remember—making love under the blankets is just not on at any time.

I know that more and more people are installing central-heating these days. If you're among these, you've no problem. If you haven't got round to it yet, choose with care an effective form of electrical heating.

A night-storage heater is the best buy, in my opinion. You don't have to remember to switch it on an hour or two before going to bed—and so risk forgetting it; it is cheap to run—about 65p a week, even at today's prices; and it keeps the room temperature just right, if you are overcome by desire at any hour of the day or night. You're also less likely to do yourself an injury than you might with an electric fire during some of your wilder cavortings off the bed.

Draughts, besides being desire-depressant if you get into their direct line of fire, also affect temperature. So see to it that the door and windows are adequately draught-proofed.

I don't know why it is that we who live in this extraordinary climate of ours are such fresh-air fiends. But don't open a window until you've finished, otherwise you won't be able to climax for buttocks and belly that are quivering for quite the wrong reasons. Besides, all your efforts to provide a good temperature will be nullified.

And, if you are erolalists, passers-by might overhear you and send for the police; or give you funny looks next time you pass them in the street.

Mirrors

Have at least one broad, long mirror fixed somewhere in the room. As many as the room will take or you can afford is an even better idea.

It's fun to have one fixed to the ceiling over the bed, though the initial outlay is a bit costly; and might make mother-in-law's eyebrows shoot up.

Why mirrors?

Because all really Sensuous Men, and quite a lot of Sensuous Women, get a really good kick out of watching themselves sexually caressing and being sexually caressed. The sight of the penis sliding in and out of the vagina turns all men on higher, and women who don't have visual kicks, generally get mental ones at the visual proof that that vibrant piston is getting up steam for the benefit of both.

Lighting

The Sensuous Couple never make love in the dark, if they can help it, because they know how stimulating the facial expressions of a turned-on partner can be, apart from the fact that if they can see where they're going, the more certain they are of arriving.

So lighting is a really important feature of any room where the Sensuous Couple frolic.

At night, you need a good light, but not a glaring

one. A lamp on either side of the bed with 100 watt bulbs and shades which cut off the direct glare is a very practical arrangement. But you also need a good centre light for your off-the-bed activities, especially mirror-watching. I suggest for this, too, a 100 watt lamp with a bowl-type opaque porcelain shade in a soft colour.

Anyhow, experiment and find out what suits you best.

No light, of course, can excel daylight. If you are not overlooked, when you have a day-time session, don't cut out the light with net curtains; let it stream unimpeded into the room. But if you are overlooked the law requires you—though not in so many words—to have net curtains, but do choose a material which lets through the most light, yet thwarts Peeping Toms, unless you like being watched. You need to know your neighbours very well to be sure that they won't dream of complaining to the authorities.

Basin

Most modern houses and apartments have H & C in all bedrooms. If the Sensuous Couple's bedroom is lacking in this respect, it would pay to have washing facilities of some kind fixed up. I will be explaining why later.

Odds and Ends

The Sensuous Couple will also need one or two other pieces of equipment.

For example, a stool at least three feet long and fourteen inches wide, with a comfortably upholstered top. It should be the exact height of the mattress when it is depressed by the Sensuous Man lying on it on his shoulders and back, his buttocks and thighs supported by the stool. (This stool makes it possible for the Sensuous Couple to use a restful woman-astride position, which allows her to have both feet firmly on the floor. This in turn allows her to make certain extremely thrilling movements which she cannot execute so expertly either kneeling or squatting astride on a non-rigid base.)

They also need another stool, this time a low one, just the right height to bring the Sensuous Man's genital area in line with the Sensuous Woman's when she lies on her back with her legs dangling over the edge of the bed. Naturally, if the bed is low enough so that this alignment happens automatically when the Sensuous Man kneels on the floor—on a cushion—this stool is superfluous.

Unless the Sensuous Couple have fairly frequent opportunities to make love in the kitchen, dining-room or breakfast-room, and like doing it on a chair, they will need a strong, comfortable chair—*without arms* —in the bedroom.

The Sensuous Couple will use a variety of aids, from creams to gadgets. If they are parents, to keep these toys from little prying eyes and to avoid embarrassing questions—a lockable drawer or chest is advisable. Even if they are not married, they should not forget there may be older prying eyes about—and most home helps I know have wonderfully flexible eyebrows, and inevitably a number of bosom friends in whose estimation they will acquire merit if they can regale friends with spicy tit-bits about their 'couple's goings-on." They won't know the details, of course, but this won't prevent them from inventing the most lurid imaginary ones if they come on clitoris ticklers or a variety of modern type *ampallangs*.*

The Sensuous Man is always attentive to the Sensuous Woman's comfort. He will, therefore, keep a good supply of large paper handkerchiefs handy so that when he withdraws he can mop up her natural lubricants, which will make her comfortable. If he also dries off his penis at the same time, this small operation has a practical significance. Stained bedsheets always have such a sordid look about them.

In Bachelor Apartments

If the Sensuous Man is a bachelor, he may live in a furnished apartment. More likely than not, his landlord will have supplied him with a single bed, and if he intends to use his bedroom as his web, there is nothing to prevent him from supplying himself with a larger bed, carefully storing away his landlord's model so that if and when he leaves for another apartment, he can replace it.

The Sensuous Bachelor should also equip his bedroom along the lines I have suggested for the Sensuous Couple.

OTHER ROOMS IN THE HOUSE

The Sensuous Couple will regard every room in the

---

* The men of some oriental tribes bore a hole through their penis just below the head and keep the quill of a feather in it, with the ends protruding a little; in other tribes, they make incisions in the skin of the penis-shaft, insert small pebbles or even little bells and let the skin grow over them. The idea is to give the woman more vaginal thrills. These objects are known as *ampallangs*. Even the most Sensuous of Men are unlikely to go to these lengths, but thoughtful manufacturers of erotic objects have devised ampallang-like objects, which can be fixed to the penis and still provide the Sensuous Woman with an extra thrill —so some say. (See Chapter 17.)

house as a potential setting for their lovemaking. No room should be barred, because different surroundings are themselves stimulating and a strong antidote to boredom.

Though I don't go in for it myself, some young friends of mine who classify themselves as a Sensuous Couple, now and again make love in the loo. When they first told me about it, I immediately thought, "Ha! There's some strange aberration like urolognia or coprophilia operating here!" (If you don't know what those two long words mean, look them up in a good sex dictionary.)

I could not have been more wrong. They had once made love in a first class loo on an Inter-Cities train and the rocking of the train as it travelled at a hundred miles an hour, had provided them with sensations they had never had before. Now they can recapture the experience in their own loo by both fantasising madly that they're in a train, helped by a cassette of train noises that they have taped.

Perhaps they do justify their classification as a Sensuous Couple, because the truly Sensuous Couple never lets an opportunity for a new experience pass by.

THE SITTING-ROOM

This room isn't used for lovemaking half as much as it should be. I know it may be difficult when there are young children about; but if you will ignore Dr Spock and follow Robert Chartham instead, you will insist on potty training from an early age, thus instilling a little self-discipline into the little blighters, so that once they are put to bed, except in an emergency, you shouldn't—in fact, won't—be bothered with them until next morning.

There must be times, too, when they are staying with Grannie, or when they are older, with friends, or when they are much older, won't be in until midnight, because they are beginning their training to become Sensuous Men and Sensuous Women.

In any case, it shouldn't be beyond the wit of Sensuous Parents to organise having the house to themselves for an hour or two every now and again.

But seriously, the Sensuous Couple should regard the sitting-room as their sex-home-from-sex (bedroom) home!

We are all too apt to go in for sex *after* we have stripped off, whereas, in fact, sex can be just as exciting, sometimes, even more so, if we start in while we've still got our clothes on, or, at any rate, most of them. (I shall be devoting quite a few pages to this technique in a moment or two.)

So, see to it that your sitting-room has a three-cushion settee, or a very roomy armchair, or, better still, both; an abundance of cushions—to be placed under buttocks, to be knelt on, to rest elbows on and so on; good lovemaking lighting; a good heating system; and any other refinement your ingenuity can conjure up. For example, a fur rug—if you like fur, and quite a number of Sensuous People find it very arousing to touch and be touched by it—makes a comfortable disporting ground and a change; while a footstool or pouffe makes a number of more esoteric positions for coupling possible.

Finally, Sensuous Parents assure that the sitting-room door can be securely locked. In the event of chance interruptions by small-fry, it is better to provoke questions than create traumas.

THE KITCHEN

Another young Sensuous Couple I know use the
kitchen almost as much as the bedroom for their lovemaking, especially on Saturday and Sunday mornings
when they haven't got to rush for the office. I think
it is probably because neither of them particularly
likes eating in bed, preferring to sit comfortably at a
table, and also because they both wake up hungry and
don't always feel like making love on an empty
stomach.

"Besides," they say, "rolling about on toast-crumbs
doesn't do anything for us."

They have net curtains at the kitchen windows, and
they keep the backdoor locked. "All the same," they
insist, "if we're involved when the milkman leaves the
pinta or we hear the paper-boy whistling up the garden path, we get a wonderful extra kick. The thought
that we might be seen, or the milkman might knock,
as he does now and again, is terrifically exciting for
both of us. We seldom climax together at other times,
maybe because we don't find it's anything special and
so don't try to organise it, but we always do when we
hear the rattle of milk bottles in his metal basket.

"We'd been doing it once standing by the sink, with
me behind June, and came just before the milkman
reached the door. He knocked, so I disengaged, as I'd
got my dressing gown on, while June hid in the corner
by the fridge. 'Cor, mate!' he exclaimed. 'Shouldn't
you be in bed. You look as if you've got a temperature
to me. . . . I've got a special offer of tinned pears.

Thought the missus might be interested.' As a matter of fact, I was still pulsing in the loins. I'd never known the sensations go on for so long before."

Quite often they sit at the breakfast table in what they call "Amiable Connection", while they eat their toast and marmalade and drink their coffee. June sits on him side-saddle to allow her easy access to the table.

When the breakfast paraphernalia has been cleared from the table, a couple of the foam seat cushions from the sitting-room settee make the table-top comfortable for June's back. Richard cut an inch off the table legs to make the alignment of the interested parties just right.

THE BATHROOM

When considering the purchase of a house or apartment the Sensuous Couple will always examine the bath most critically. No bath should be shorter than five foot six; six foot is preferable; six foot six sybaritic.

It must be capable of taking a recumbent couple without pinching either at the hips; and deep enough to allow both to be covered by water when they lie in it layered.

An air-cushion or a soft foam support for the Sensuous Man's head and either a rectangular one or two square ones for placing under each of his shoulder blades—they can be bought in attractive patterns and colours—make all the difference to an in-bath encounter. A fourth cushion, to be placed at the base of his spine, is sheer luxury; but the Sensuous Couple should always pamper themselves when they can.

(I'll discuss ways and means in Chapter 8.)

No truly Sensuous Couple's bathroom will be without its shower. It must have a very strong jet of water, and be thermostatically controlled. Some prefer a hand-shower, for reasons which will become evident when we consider techniques. The only drawback of the hand-shower is that many are not convertible from spray to jet. Such convertibles, however, can be found.

In a sentence, every nook and cranny in the house which has anything that commends itself to an ingenious imagination is acceptable to the Sensuous Couple as love-settings.

CHAPTER THREE

TIME AND TIMING

Any time is loving-time to the Sensuous Couple. But. . . .

To my way of thinking, the planned session ought never to last less than one hour, preferably an hour and a half, ideally, two hours or more.

I say *planned* session to differentiate it from the more spontaneous session i.e. those sessions which come about when one is least expecting them, sparked off by a fortuitous caress, a gesture, a look, a word, when all of a sudden the serpent of sex stirs in the loins, uncoils and prepares to strike. This usually happens sometime after one has been in bed, during the middle of the night, on a workday morning or maybe at lunchtime, when there just isn't time to spare.

The majority of couples, unsensuous as well as sensuous ones, make love on average between twelve and sixteen times a month. From a recent inquiry into the nature of the sex-drive which I have carried out with the co-operation of a hundred couples spanning most age-groups between twenty and sixty-five, half of all copulations are in response to the sex-drive, the other half being cold-bloodedly—though that seems a strange word to associate with it—provoked.

In other words, at least half the time most couples do not wait for the body chemistry to nudge them into action, but just the reverse, they nudge the body chemistry into action.

There is a certain danger in this arrangement of a couple getting into a set time-pattern of timing—Tuesdays, Thursdays, Saturdays and Sundays, for example. The trouble is that the social round—in which I include work and bringing up a family in a well-run household—favours the time-pattern. But except for Saturdays and Sundays, the regular setting apart of certain afternoons and evenings should be avoided like the plague.

I think that most couples who take their lovemaking seriously—and this, of course, includes all Sensuous Couples—realise this, and that it is this realisation that urges so many to plan a session outside the rhythm of the body chemistry.

Let me try to explain this a little bit more. The body chemistry i.e. the sex-drive, works to a certain pattern, or rhythm, rather like the woman's monthly cycle. It differs in various individuals, and things can happen which will upset the rhythm, but as an example of

what I mean; the young, healthy, average-sexed man
has a three-day rhythm. That is to say, if he has a
love-session on Monday night which empties his
seminal vesicles of fluid and sperms and his prostate
gland of its fluid, and he then doesn't have any
kind of sexual activity until Thursday, by Thursday
his seminal vesicles and his prostate gland will be
straining at the leash again, and if he has a go on
Thursday night, he will emit his maximum volume of
ejaculate and his maximum sperm-count, with his first
orgasm that night.

I am not saying that the fullness of seminal vesicles
and prostate are what prompts the man to seek a
sexual outlet, that they regulate his sex-drive. They
have something to do with it, but it's a bit more com-
plicated than that, and I needn't bore you with it here.

However, it does illustrate what I am trying to get
over—that the sex-drive works to a time pattern that
is more or less regular. If one responds only to the
sex-drive, therefore, one immediately establishes a
pattern of love-sessions, even though, over a period,
one would be making love on different days of the
week.

Fortunately, both men and women don't have to wait
for their sex-drives to operate. They can fuck whenever they have a mind to, provided the man hasn't any
hang-ups that prevent his penis from getting stiff
under direct manipulation of fingers or mouth, and
the woman's vagina can't be relaxed enough, because
she may not be roused, for the penis to get into it
with the aid of saliva. But any Sensuous Woman can,
like the male, be roused at will if her partner is a Sensuous Man.

Every Sensuous Couple can recognise sex-drive

promptings when they experience them. That tenseness in the loins and genitals, that pleasant sensation of interior fullness which indicates that something, somewhere has got to be emptied, which are experienced as a gradual build-up, at one time reaching a pitch where they impinge on the consciousness, but which is not the peak of the build-up taken as a whole. In other words, you get due warning.

This warning can come at any time of the day, and when it does you know for a certainty that within a short time you're going to be on the job. It is the inevitability of this which allows you to *plan* the timing of your session, having taken into consideration what has to be done—get home from the office, get the children to bed—before you can get down to it.

In this sense, too, the deliberate session can be a planned session if you say to yourself sometime beforehand, though without any prompting from your body chemistry, "I wouldn't mind getting down to it tonight."

I haven't had the opportunity to analyse completely my sex-drive material, but what I have done convinces me that the deliberate session is the saving grace of human copulatory activity; and on this basis I commend it to all Sensuous Couples, though I feel pretty certain they will have made the discovery for themselves, unconsciously if not consciously.

One thing I probably ought to point out to forestall my more niggling critics: There are not many couples in the world whose sex-drive rhythms coincide. So often, the Sensuous Man will be responding to sex-drive promptings while his Sensuous Partner is not, and vice versa. But this doesn't matter. Love making is an equal partnership. Both have the right to initiate

activities, and with Sensuous Couples, both have the
right to expect the other to co-operate.

Although one partner has made up his/her mind
that there must be a session before the day is out, the
Sensuous Couple don't announce it to one another beforehand. That would be too clinically deliberate.
They make their desires known to one another by ges-
tures and caresses, so that when the time comes a hint
of an early bed, or a caress that means business here
and now, doesn't come as too great a surprise.

"Who the hell can afford two hours for a session?"

The Sensuous Couple will make sure that they can.
Of course, it won't always be possible, because the
days are always so full and the hectic demands of our
hectic lives necessitate the recuperation of several
hours sleep. But the self-respecting Sensuous Couple
will make the time as often as is feasible. More often
than not, it's merely a matter of forgoing a favourite
TV programme.

An hour and a half can frequently be found; an
hour is always possible.

But why so long?

A few pages back I wrote, "The Sensuous Couple
embark on every session determined to give each other
the greatest sexual thrill they've ever had. They do so,
because they are using their penis and vagina, their
mouths, and their hands and any other parts of their
bodies to assure their minds that their love for each
other is genuine and deep."

You can't, or at least you shouldn't try, to hurry
any woman, and any woman who lets herself be hurried cannot honestly claim to be a Sensuous Woman.

Equally, no man can claim to be a Sensuous Man
unless he can control absolutely his speed to orgasm.

I know many men will think I'm talking nonsense, but honestly it can be done. It may take time and patience, but it is within the eventual scope of all except the psychologically hung-up too rapid ejaculator or partially impotent. And it doesn't mean either, that his partner is not to caress him at all, or even only half-heartedly. He should be able to take all she can provide in the way of stimulation.

A man very well known to me can make love to a Sensuous Woman and be made love to by her for any length of time, and though he may at times be close to the boil, he can always be sure he is not going to boil over until he gives himself permission to do so. He can pass an hour, after a long session of fellatio and other exciting activities, with his penis in a vagina, and, what's more, keep up a constant movement, and still not come. When he is sure that his partner is satisfied—and if he's not sure, he will ask her—he tells her, "I'm going to come now!" and he does in ten, fifteen, thirty seconds!

He doesn't do it by reciting a poem, or thinking about that snag on such and such a job at work, or by smoking a cigarette, or reading a book, or any such gimmick. By a kind of self-hypnotism, he has trained his body to respond only to the commands of his mind. He's an experienced man, admittedly; he's in late middle-age; and he's been fucking since he was 13. But he's absolutely certain that this is well within the reach of every man, who is prepared to make the effort.

I would like to recommend a little booklet on this very subject which has recently come my way. It's called *Ejaculation Control Techniques* by Robin Saxon, obtainable from the author, whose address I will pass to anyone interested. The advice given in it is much sounder and more effective than the suggestions made in *The Sensuous Man* by "M".

And here is a practical tip which has come my way from my study of too rapid ejaculators. During this study I discovered that all too-rapid ejaculators begin to thrust with buttock-muscles tensed as soon as they get the penis in position. It hadn't struck me before that tensed buttock-muscles had any connection with speed to orgasm, but a brief analysis of my own techniques soon showed that a significant part of the secret of delaying orgasm lies in relaxed pelvic- and buttock-muscles. Unconsciously, so I found out, I had been using the technique of relaxed buttock- and pelvic-muscles for delaying orgasm and of tensing them when I wanted to come.

My very, very good friend confirmed the necessity for this. "When I have decided I'm going to come," he told me, "I can control the speed with which I come by the degree with which I clench my buttock- and pelvic-muscles. Really tight—ten seconds; not quite so tight—fifteen seconds; and a shade more relaxed still—thirty seconds."

Sexologists use one word for the action of the penis in the vagina—thrust. I used to myself. I don't any longer. With pelvic- and buttock-muscles relaxed I describe the movement as "swinging"; when these muscles are tensed, then the man is "thrusting."

I am quite sure that all Sensuous Men have discovered this for themselves; but I thought I would mention it.

But still the cry goes up—"Why an hour, an hour and a half, why, in heck, two hours?"

I thought we had agreed that the Sensuous Couple

make love with the view to obtaining the most intense sensual experience their bodies and techniques will allow, and that you hope to come off with such an orgasm that you will be out of this world—and I mean, out of this world—for a few gloriously, ecstatically, exquisite moments?

All right then, there is a practical reason for the length of time you devote to your sessions. It's this!

The more you are stimulated, the more intensely you will climax. And the technique the Sensual Couple use is this. They bring each other to the threshold of coming; pause till they are relaxed again; begin stimulation once more to the same point; pause again.

The more often both the Sensuous Woman and the Sensuous Man are brought to the threshold of coming, when they do decide at last to come the more devastating the orgasm will be.

Lovemaking, therefore, can't be hurried if you want to know what a real orgasm is like. And I do assure you, once you do know, you'll never be satisfied with less.

The Sensuous Man can be brought to the threshold at least six times an hour; the Sensuous Woman at least four times. To do this, the Sensuous Man must have the absolute control I was talking about a few moments ago, but when he finally does go over the edge it will all have been worth it. If the couple make love for two hours he can come to his petit climax (the threshold) twelve times. Each petit climax more he has, means that the grand climax (orgasm) when it at last arrives, will be the more ecstatic. So it is, too, with the Sensuous Woman, who will have taught herself to respond to stimulation until she can, if she works that hard at it, have as many petit climaxes as her Sensuous Partner.

This is why you must have time, except, as I have said, on those comparatively rare occasions when both are on the point of coming before they've started. The grand climax then can be—in fact, invariably is— absolutely wild; and such occasions are good. But it is only on such occasions that the slam-bam is justified. I've found, even so, that wild though the climax is, there is nearly always an urge to begin another, more leisurely, session after a short pause.

As for timing: as I have said, any time is love-time for the Sensuous Couple. But just a hint of advice. Don't go in for violent antics after a heavy meal!

If you do use dinner as an aid to seduction, choose the food with care. If at home and the Sensuous Wife has fed you, she will have seen to it that you have eaten wisely. Nevertheless, time things so that you have your orgasm not less than two hours after you've finished eating.

Coupling puts quite a demand on heart and lungs. Someone has calculated that it's the equivalent to the exertion of running 100 metres in 11 seconds, and no one would do that after a heavy meal, except a true dolt. You may think you are getting away with it when you are young, but you are really laying up trouble for yourself later on. When you're fifty-five or sixty, you wouldn't like to put your Sensuous Partner in the embarrassing situation of having a coronary while you're coupled would you?

Scientifically speaking—and I'm not joking—the ideal time for a session is between 6 a.m. and 8 a.m. It has been discovered that most men's daily production cycle of testosterone—the hormone that among other things makes him feel randy—is at its peak at 7 a.m.

The Sensuous Couple, however, will vary the time, as they do the place, to get variety into their love-lives and so avoid an encounter with that vicious love-killer, boredom.

CHAPTER 4

COMMUNICATING

It would not surprise me if statistics proved that next after sexual boredom, lack of communication between partners was the cause of the breakdown of marriage. In fact, I would go further, and say it was the first cause, since boredom could not possibly continue if the couple would say they were bored and discuss why they were bored.

I appreciate that the language of sex is a drawback to spontaneous frank talk about sex, but if a man is going to put his penis into the woman, and she wants him to put it in, they can't get much more intimate and close than that, so there ought not to be any great difficulty in talking about it.

Over and over again, men and women begin their letters to me with an apology. "I'm afraid I don't know the right words to use, so I hope you will excuse me if I may seem crude or can't express myself properly, and I do hope you will also be able to understand what I am trying to say."

What these people are really trying to tell me is that

penis and *vagina* are too posh for them to use—they know these words because I use them in my books, and they are writing to me because they have read my books—and at the same time are themselves too posh to use *cock* and *cunt*.

For many of the sex-words, which are very artificial for the most part, it should not be beyond the wit of any couple to invent words of their own. We can get rid of "ejaculation" for a start, by using "shooting" —which is how the semen leaves the penis—and "orgasm" by using "coming," "coming off." "Love-making" is a good substitute for "sexual intercourse" and "coitus"; "coupling" is much more human than "intromission" and "penetration". "Balls", I think, is now quite a widely acceptable synonym for "testicles plus scrotum". So we are left with "penis," "clitoris," and "vagina".

I am all in favour of the four-letter words, and hope one day they will regain their respectability. Nothing would please me more than to use them habitually in this book, but out of deference to my publisher's wishes, I feel I must hypocritically restrain myself. You may have noticed, however, that one or two "fucks" have slipped in already. They have, because the word seems to me the real *mot juste* in that particular passage. Read those lines again and see if you don't agree with me that the substitution of even "making love" or "lovemaking" would emasculate my style at those points.

English men are the main culprits in the slow universal acceptance of the vernacular terms. They use the words themselves when they are being their most ribald about sex, and since women are too sensitive creatures to be subjected to ribaldry, a man feels he would not be a gentleman if he said to a lady, "You've a wonderful cunt! How do you feel about my cock?"

I've told the story once or twice before, of the man who approached me one day with a problem. He confided that he had a strong desire during a half-minute or so before coming off, for his partner gently to hold his balls.

"She wouldn't object, would she?" I asked.

"Of course not," he said.

"Then why don't you ask her?"

"But that's the problem! You can't ask a woman 'to hold your balls', and I'd feel a proper Charlie if I whispered in her shell-like ear, 'Hold my testicles, darling!' "

We had quite an argument about it, which he eventually concluded by saying, with grievous disappointment, "I thought if anyone knew, you would." I hadn't the heart not to tell him, "Well, why say anything? Why not just take her hand and put your balls in it?"

He brightened at once. "I'd never thought of that. Thanks."

It's all on a par with "nice women don't smoke cigarettes in the street." I don't think women—or men —should smoke cigarettes at all, but if they smoke in the house I can't for the life of me see any difference in behaviour if they smoke in the street.

There is a similar reluctance to use the four-letter words on the part of women, who feel that to do so would be to breach the illusive myth of female modesty.

But the Sensuous Woman knows that if she is going to be really sensuous, she must throw female modesty overboard. How can such a fantastic human experience as whole-hearted response to sex be circumscribed by modesty? So, if she can give full range to her actions, I don't see why she can't use one or two words and phrases that happen to have been debased by men without being immodest. I am sure that if women began a campaign to use these words when they have sex, the words would soon be restored to respectability and general usage.

However, if a couple really cannot bring themselves to use four-letter words during the intimacy of sex, then they will have to invent euphemisms of their own—for talk to one another they must. No man can become a Sensuous Man, no woman a Sensuous Woman, no couple a Sensuous Couple, until they are able to talk to their partners freely of their own sexual needs, likes and dislikes and discuss freely their partner's requirements, too.

This talking together has got nothing to do either with erolalia or erotolalia. It is just ordinary straightforward communication. How essential such communication is, is probably only brought home to people who deal with the sexual problems of others.

A woman complains to me that she has never had an orgasm during penis-vagina contact. Her husband can keep going inside her for five, often ten, minutes, but she can't come in that time and always has to be finished off by hand or mouth.

In all cases of delayed orgasm, now that I've finally learned some sense, the first question I ask is, "Who decides when your partner puts his penis into you— you or him?"

This particular woman gave what has almost become the stock answer, because it is so frequently given, "He does."

"Does he ask you if you are ready?"

"No, but I wish he would, because I always feel I'd like him to go on stimulating me a bit more before he does come in me."

"Why don't you ask him to stimulate you a bit more, then?"

"Oh, we don't talk about sex."

The man who wanted his balls held was on the verge of becoming obsessed by it. (Frustrations nearly always turn into obsessions.) Yet all he had to do was to tell his partner what he wanted. When I saw him again a week or two later, I asked him if he'd done anything about it. "Certainly," he grinned, and went on, "but what really riles me is the thought of all those years lost when I could have been enjoying it."

"You can always make up for lost time," I suggested.

"How?"

"Make love more often."

"You do have all the answers, don't you?" he said, and I couldn't tell whether he was being facetious or grateful.

The sex-books say that almost all women are very responsive to having their nipples rolled between fingers and thumb. Almost all men read this as "*all* women." But there are women whose response to this technique is irritation rather than arousal.

One woman came to me because she was worried that her reaction might mean that she was abnormal.

"It just tickles," she said. "What really turns me on is to have my partner hold my breast in his hand, and squeeze it hard."

"Have you told him how you feel and what you would like him to do?"

"I haven't liked to, in case he should think I was kinky."

"Well, you're not. So tell him, and if he thinks you're funny, tell him to come and see me."

For goodness knows how long, she had been putting up with real discomfort from a technique which her partner used on her in all good faith, simply because they had not learned to communicate! It's so ridiculous, when all that is needed is confidence in the partner and three or four spoken words.

Another gazed at a picture above my head while she told me, "I had an affair some years ago with a man who liked to rub his penis-head on my nipple until he came. It was the wildest sensation I've ever had. I used to come, too, as soon as I felt the first spurt drowning my nipple. I long for my husband to do it."

"Have you asked him to?"

"Oh, no! It's not the sort of thing one can ask one's husband to do, is it?"

"Why ever not?"

"I would feel it was very immodest."

"Do you and your husband talk about sex?"

"A bit. But it's not very easy."

"But you are talking to me quite happily about it, aren't you?"

"But you're different. You understand."

"I'm a stranger. I would have thought it would be easier to talk to a man who is more intimate with you than any other man."

"I know it should be like that. But we don't really need to talk a lot about it."

"But you really do need to!"

After a pause, while she studied the picture more

carefully, she asked, "I don't suppose you could do anything about it—have a word with my husband, I mean?"

"Yes, I could, but I don't see why I should. You can speak to him quite as clearly as I."

"But you would be able to sound him out first, to see whether he would object."

"Is he a prude, then?"

"No, but you must admit it's rather a strange way of getting turned on."

"Not at all. There are thousands of women who get the sort of thrill out of this particular activity as you do."

Soft-hearted me, I spoke to the husband. Far from having any objections, he was delighted. "I've been wondering for quite a while now what we could do that was new. Why didn't she tell me herself?"

"I gather you don't talk to one another much about sex."

"No, not much."

"Well, I suggest you begin right away talking more often. You don't know what else you might be missing."

They had been married for four years, and in all that time she had denied herself pleasure because she would not speak a few very brief words; and he had been missing out, too, for the same reason.

The sex-books say that the massively nerve-packed frenum—the little band of skin which joins the skin of the shaft of the penis to the membrane covering its head, on the underside—is the most sensitive spot on the whole penis. For the majority of men, it probably is, but for quite a significant number, for one reason or another, the frenum is almost dead. Among these men their most sensitive spot may be either the rim of the opening, or the few square millimetres just below the opening, or the edge of the rim which the penis-head forms with the shaft, or the groove under the rim.

A young man who came to see me about retarded ejaculation—he could not reach climax even if he moved his penis in the vagina without stopping, for an hour or more; in fact, it took him over an hour of continuous direct stimulation of his penis by his partner to come, and that was only on comparatively rare occasions; very often he couldn't climax at all. This young man revealed under my probing that he had scarcely any feeling at all in his frenum and penis-head.

His difficulty had psychological causes, but I asked him whether he ever brought himself off and how long it usually took him.

"Oh, four or five minutes."

"How do you masturbate?"

"Well, I find that the underside of my penis for about an inch and a half from the base is very sensitive. I lie on my back and rub this spot with two finger-tips."

"Does your partner know about this?"

"No."

"Why not?"

"I haven't told her."

"Why haven't you?"

"I don't know, really. We don't talk much about sex."

"Do you think you might come more easily if she used your technique?"

"I don't see why not. But what I find is so bloody

frustrating is not being able to come off while I'm in her."

"Now you've told me your little secret, I might be able to suggest something that would let you do just that. Lie on your back, with her lying on her back on you; or, it might be more comfortable if you slouched down rather on the settee and she mounted you with her back to you. In these two positions, those vital one and a half inches can't get into her vagina. If she rubs you there with her finger-tips in the way you do yourself, I'm pretty certain you will climax in much less time than it takes you now."*

The Sensuous Man and the Sensuous Woman will be able to confirm what I have been saying, and the Sensuous Couple will discover very quickly what a time-saver communicating is.

Normally it can take ages before a couple can begin to swing along together, if they adopt the only alternative method—"Trial and Error." Mind you, Trial and Error is the only way for a couple who have not yet learned to be a Sensuous Man and a Sensuous Woman to get to know one another sexually. But even so, if they *will* talk, they can cut down considerably the time it takes to turn themselves into a Sensuous Couple.

The would-be Sensuous Man and Sensuous Woman are bound to be sexually imaginative; they can't help it. They wouldn't set out to be these highly desirable creatures if they hadn't the initial impetus of imagina-

---

* It worked; but what is more, the fact that he was able to climax while he was up her, unblocked him psychologically, and he was soon able to function in any position. It took only a couple of weeks, instead of the lengthy psychotherapy he would have had to undergo otherwise—and with no guarantee of success.

tion and the lack of all inhibitions, which would undoubtedly block the efforts of the imagination to translate theory into practice, if they existed.

So, since they are sexually imaginative, the Sensuous Man and the Sensuous Woman are more than likely to have various little tricks of their own invention up their sleeves, especially so if they are Sensuous Men and Sensuous Women of experience.

But the Sensuous Couple, in their first encounter especially, will avoid a lot of recriminations or disappointments if they have a chat about likes and dislikes before they get down to business. It saves time later, if each partner knows that as far as the other is concerned, such-and-such draws no arousal responses, that this-and-that is sexually deflating, or that so-and-so sends them wild.

The Sensuous Couple are never satisfied. Even after they've been working at a regular relationship for several years, they regard themselves still in the experimental stage. But it's no use experimenting on another person if you don't know how the experiment is working either way; and you can't find out unless you ask and are told.

How can a Sensuous Man know that his Sensuous Partner enjoys three fingers exploring her vagina, but not two or one, unless she tells him? How can a Sensuous Woman who once had a partner who was sent wild by the gentlest of love-nips on the scrotum know, unless he tells her, that her Sensuous Partner finds the gentlest love-nips on the scrotum excruciatingly painful, but adores quite sharp love-nips on the tip of his foreskin when it's pulled right forward? (There are such Sensuous Men with foreskins, who do find this particular caress very exciting!)

There is another use for talking, too.

Lots of Sensuous Couples are, or may be capable of being, turned on by listening to each other recounting in considerable detail, past sexual exploits. No Sensuous Man or Woman can use this technique unless they have the words and the freedom from inhibitions to speak them. Similarly, no Sensuous Couple let any opportunity of arousal slip through their fingers for want of being prepared.

Words, not necessarily taboo words, come into erolalia, too. If a couple are not accustomed to talking to one another at all, they will find it very difficult to become erolalists. They will be missing out on something which I think is an interesting and exciting sexual activity, and I hope that when they have read what I have to say about it later, all will agree with me.

No Sensuous Couple will willingly miss out on anything at all. They know that one sure way to avoid doing so is to communicate.

CHAPTER FIVE

SENSITIVITY EXPLORING EXERCISES

TO THE SENSUOUS COUPLE

I've said it before, but I'll say it again: The whole secret of being a really successful Sensuous Lover is to know the response potential of every square millimetre of your partner's body, and to have the partner as familiar with yours.

The art of physical sex is based on physical sensation; not on one sensation, but on a combination of many; not on one level but in a crescendoing build-up, eventually to explode in orgasm.

With the best will in the world and the greatest skill, no one can learn a body in the detail that it needs to be known if either partner is to be correctly classified as a Sensuous Lover, in a couple of hours. You will see, of course, at once, what this means!

It means that the genuinely sincere Sensuous Man and Sensuous Woman will not expect to qualify as a Sensuous Couple in one session. This also means that the Sensuous Man and the Sensuous Woman will not go in for the casual encounter except for the want of something better. Even if they have no intention of forming a quasi-permanent relationship, but still want to give to and get from one another the best, they will set up a series of sessions.

I am not for one moment suggesting that the Casual Encounter won't be well worth while. The conjunction of Sensuous Man and Sensuous Woman can never fail to be very interesting and satisfying, but for lack of time it can never be the tops.

The Sensuous Man and the Sensuous Woman are able to recognise other Sensuous Men and other Sensuous Women, if not on sight, then at least within a few caresses. So that is some time saved.

I was going to say that a Sensuous Man doesn't waste time on a non-Sensuous Woman, and vice versa, but, of course, that's not on, because unless the partner is as cold as the ice-pack, which one American counsellor advises the woman to clamp on her partner's balls just as he's beginning to come, she won't be able entirely to resist him.

Besides, there is also the point that the Sensuous Man needs to show off from time to time, and the Sensuous Woman to give her partner something to remember her by, and it is easier to make an impression on a not-so-sensuous partner. In these encounters there cannot fail to be a degree of physical satisfaction, but the real reward is the look of bewildered appreciation that sex can be so fantastic—as it cannot fail to be for them, though the Sensuous One has played it in a low key on this occasion.

But otherwise, whenever possible, the Sensuous Man will select, or find himself selected by, a Sensuous Woman.

This being so, the next time-saver is what a Sensuous Friend of mine does first time round with a new partner. Having got her on the bed he takes her in his arms and asks, "Is there anything you particularly don't like?" and notes very carefully what she says.

Then he says, "I don't like having my navel tickled with a finger-tip or the tongue-tip, for that matter; and heavy breathing in my left ear, turns me right off."

("Sometimes they look a bit surprised," he says, "because funnily enough I've met some Sensuous Women who overlook the navel as a sensitive zone, and put me down as odd, which maybe I am, because breathing in my earhole makes me shiver.")

Next he asks, "Is there anything you particularly like?" then tells them, "having my buttocks squeezed really hard just as I come sends me wild."

"These little exchanges," he says, "clear the ground considerably. Nothing puts a chap off more than to be told in the middle of one of his patent caresses, 'Don't do that, I don't like it!' and one avoids discomfort oneself if one tells them what one doesn't like, and gives oneself *some* pleasure at least by telling them what one does like."

He gave me that tip forty-three years ago—he's a bit older than me, and still at it—and I can personally vouch for every word of it.

Having made this exchange, one can get down to business.

By the way, I am addressing myself from this point on to the Sensuous Man and the Sensuous Woman who intend the first encounter to be one of a series, or to develop into a permanent Sensuous Couple.

SENSITIVITY EXPLORING EXERCISE NO. 1

Lying side by side naked on the bed, scrutinise each other's body so that you get to know what it looks like. There will be times when you are making certain caresses when you won't be able to see much of him/ her, but if you've got a mental photograph it's quite a help in imagining how he/she is enjoying what you're doing; and you really need to know that, because it encourages you to even greater heights of skill.

Make sure that both have removed watches and rings—except wedding rings—and the Sensuous Woman necklaces, bracelets and umbilical diamonds or rubies.

POINTS TO LOOK FOR

The Woman
Look at his ears and see if he has well-formed lobes.

If he has you can be pretty sure he likes to have them nibbled.

Inspect his nipples. If they stand out well from the areola and are fairly big, you can be fairly certain that they are sensitive, and will repay the attentions of finger, lips and tongue. But it is my belief that all men can be trained to nipple-sensitivity, so a little later on you can go to work on them, stretching and enlarging them.

Regard his penis carefully. He's also certain to have an erection by this time, but if he hasn't encourage one. When it's nicely upstanding (as the Rotarians say), size up its dimensions. You don't have to worry about its thickness, but length may be important to you if you are not one of those women—and there are a lot about—who find accommodating the whole of an 8-inch specimen a bit uncomfortable. You will make a note not to encourage him to take up those coupling positions which allow the whole length to go in.

(If you are not very good on guessing lengths, the second joint of the fore-finger on the right hand of most women is roughly one inch long. Run this joint up his penis along the top side, from pubic bone to tip, and you will have a rough idea how long his peter is. Near enough to tell you whether you are going to be happy engulfing it or not.)

If his penis is a bit below average length and you don't want him to be discouraged by it, you will help him if you make more use of those coupling positions which you would avoid for the 8-inch model.

No matter how long it is, if it is particularly slim, make a note to test your Vaginal Sphincter Squeezing Technique, and see that it is in really good shape. If you've recently been accustomed to a bulky intruder, you may have let this very useful muscle get just a little slack.

Take note whether he has a paunch and if so, how protuberant it is, because it can affect the depth of his penis-penetration-potential in all but a few positions, and you will have to make allowances for that.

If he is not circumcised, inspect his foreskin. If it's already right back behind the rim, you've nothing to worry about, but if it is fully or half-covering the penis-head, test whether it slips right back easily. Many a girl has caused a man excruciating pain by trying to force back a tight foreskin.

Size up the dimensions of his balls. He won't mind your doing it manually. If they're a bit outsize or you've got a cupid-bow mouth, you will send him up to the ceiling when you try to get them both into your mouth at once.

Clasp his penis firmly at the base with the whole of your hand and draw the hand up to the head. If a drop or two of his gland fluid doesn't appear at the tip, more likely than not he'll need a little extra lubrication— saliva—before he goes into you. Sensuous Man that he is, he will almost certainly be aware of this particular need and attend to it himself, but it's just as well to check that he does, first time round.

The Man

Have a good look at the lobes of her ears. If she hasn't any it will be a waste of time to try and nibble them.

If her breasts are on the bulky side, there are certain breast-stimulating techniques you won't be able to use.

If her thighs are on the heavy side and you are not

all that slim either, note to ask her to bring up her knees to her breasts before you try to go in her, otherwise you may lose precious seconds at a vital moment manoeuvring your penis into position.

Ask her kindly to spread her legs; raise yourself on an elbow; with the fingers part her outer lips and locate her clitoris. Estimate its size—not that size counts much, or anything at all sensitivity-wise—because you will then be able to get an idea of the techniques that will be most effective. (I've only encountered one clitoris so long that one could work on it as though it were a nipple, and the erolalia of the owner and the feel of it between one's lips were so fantastic that it made my penis ache. I've never forgotten it, and I'm still on the look-out for another. If you come across one, and everything else seems hopeless, don't for heaven's sake, pass it up! Don't be a dog-in-the-manger either, about it. Drop me a line; I'll do the same for you if I have any luck!)

While on your clitoral tour of inspection, find out whether the hood retracts easily. If it does, you're not likely to encounter any stimulation snags. If it is "buried", you may have to experiment, because "buried" clitorises are inclined to be somewhat individualistic.

Ask her to show you *how* she likes her clitoris to be manually stimulated. Preferences are almost as numerous as women, and only she—unless she's a very extraordinary woman and doesn't know herself—can show you.

I think, too, that it's useful to note the growth of the hair in the clitoral region. Personally, I don't go much for getting a mouthful of hair when I'm interested in something smoother. If her outer lips are a bit too hirsute in your opinion, offer to clip the hair for her.

Talking about hair, look at the hair on her head. If it is well coiffeured, you have little to worry about. But if it is "floppy" you would be within your rights to suggest that she might wear a bandeau when she is on the bed with you. There are some caressing conjunctions in which the cranial hair of your partner can make all the difference between success and failure.

Next, slip your hand behind one of her knees, as if by accident. Touch it lightly and note her reactions. If she has the same sort of reflex action that healthy people have when you strike them just below the kneecap with a toffee hammer, you will know that you are in for a whale of a time, and play up accordingly.

SENSITIVITY EXPLORING EXERCISE NO. 2

The Woman

Ask him to get off the bed for a moment, and stand up straight.

Note the angle his penis makes with his belly. The nearer the tip is to his navel, the longer he will be able to ride you, and that is useful to know. This does not apply to those over the age of 40 who have been Sensuous Men for at least ten years, because though their penises stand more horizontally than the young man's normally does, they have learned the control to ride you for ever, if that's what you want.

The Man

Put a finger in her vagina. Ask her to grip it. If you can't feel her gripping, put in two, then if necessary, three.

If you can feel her grip on one finger, you can be sure she can drive you really wild if she wants to.

If you can't feel anything when you put four fingers in, you can be sure that you haven't enticed a Sensuous Woman onto your bed.

SENSITIVITY EXPLORING EXERCISE NO. 3

The Woman

While he is still standing beside the bed, notice the hang of his balls.

If they are drawn right up tight and firm under his penis, you'll know he hasn't come for thirty-six hours at least, and that it is going to be quite a session.

If they hang slightly slack, you can be almost certain that you are in for a nice, slow, but nevertheless, really exciting ride.

The Man

Get your face between her legs and your tongue into her vagina. Draw your tongue rapidly in and out.

If she arches her back, you may be sure she will come more than once.

SENSITIVITY EXPLORING EXERCISE NO. 4

The Woman

Suck his big toe. It doesn't matter on which foot.

If he squirms or groans, you can be sure you are on to a winner.

The Man

Suck her big toe. It doesn't matter on which foot.

If she squirms or groans, you can be sure that you can pull out all the stops and be thoroughly appreciated.

SENSITIVITY EXPLORING EXERCISE NO. 5

The Woman
Ask him to lie on his belly. With two finger-tips, beginning at the base of the spine, move up his backbone inch by inch, pressing lightly each time, until you have covered about four inches.

If at one point, his buttocks buck, you can be sure you have found his Erection Centre.

This knowledge is extremely useful, because if he flags now and again you can stiffen him up again in no time by a little pressure on this point. Not only that, you can be sure that he will take to you tremendously, because not many women, even Sensuous Women, can find the vital spot.

The Man
Ask her to lie on her belly.

Beginning at the nape of her neck, run the tip of your tongue down the length of her spine.

If she lifts her buttocks to meet your tongue as you reach the small of her back, you may be certain that she has a very high degree of overall sensitivity, which is invaluable to know at the first meeting.

SENSITIVITY EXPLORING EXERCISE NO. 6

Both
Each should try out on the other the special

caresses they particularly like, and explore any personal highly sensitive zones.

During this mutual experimenting, each partner should give the other the fullest help and guidance.

This exercise has the effect of bringing the couple into quite intimate terms in a short time. Once you have shared your sex secrets with somebody else your relationship must inevitably be closer; your emotional rapport will get off on the right footing, too.

These half-dozen Sensitivity Exploring Exercises are designed, as I have said, to allow the Sensuous Man and the Sensuous Woman making love for the first time, to discover each other's sensitivity potential in the shortest possible time, and so save precious minutes for the more serious business of working one another up, and becoming a Sensuous Couple.

The fact that they are already Sensuous Men and Sensuous Women means that they are sexually imaginative. They may, therefore, have exercises which they have devised themselves, and they should not hesitate to use them.

One of the most important things to remember about sex is that scarcely any two people respond in *exactly* the same way. That's what makes it such fun.

CHAPTER SIX

UNDRESSING AS FOREPLAY

Every now and again I ask around, "Do you ever undress one another as part of your foreplay?" More often than not I am received with blank looks, or I am told, "Well, when she's undressing I sometimes help her off with her panties and bra."

In fact, undressing one another can be very exciting, and I would recommend all those who haven't yet tried it, to give it a go. It isn't an "every time" technique, because it isn't always convenient, since the place for it is the sitting-room settee. But even if it is used only infrequently it can make a welcome change from the more usual session in which the first encounters are made when the couple are already nude.

You need not restrict it, either, to the from-start-to-orgasm-sitting-room-session. You can begin a session with it, which will, sometime after the couple have stripped off, be transferred to the bedroom for the Third Act and the Grand Finale.

In my view, undressing as foreplay requires certain prerequisites. Nothing can be more turning off than a tie which doesn't untie easily, a bra that doesn't unclip at a touch, a button that chips a finger-nail in the unbuttoning, and so on. These can all be avoided if the couple take care with their dressing beforehand.

"But if the tie is removed, buttons are undone, shoes and socks taken off," I can hear someone protest, "Surely that is going to take away the spontaneity of lovemaking which, all Sensuous Couples agree, is what gives the session that special indefinable quality which makes the act human rather than animal."

I agree with the superiority of spontaneity over deliberateness (which seems so cold-blooded), but I do suggest that deliberateness, when sparingly used, can be one of those variations which are designed to prevent boredom overcasting one's sex-life. As a matter of fact, undressing as foreplay need not be deliberate except on those occasions when either he or she suggests a strip-session in the afternoon. Since most strip-sessions will take place in the evenings, the Sensuous Couples, who are always prepared for anything to happen, will be prepared for this.

In any case, sex or no sex, the evening after a day at the office or ten hours of household chores is always more relaxing if the dress is more casual than it might be if you had friends coming in. Let me offer you a few suggestions.

First for the man. If he is in the habit of wearing an undervest during the day, if the heating-system of the sitting room is what it should be, it will be a superfluous garment for the evening. So when he goes up to change on arriving home, he will take it off. I suggest this, because all garments that are taken off over the head are awkward to remove during foreplay. Pullovers come into this category, so he should go in for cardigans; so do all shirts, except tunic shirts, which button right through down the front.

An open-necked shirt with a silk handkerchief or scarf tied loosely round the neck, does away with the tie. Under his cardigan he should have his shirt cuffs unfastened.

I don't advise jeans, because they are usually tight-fitting round the lower legs, and can be a devil to pull off. Instead, he should wear loosely fitting trousers which he can step out of when, the waistband and zip having been undone, he stands up and they fall about his feet.

Unless he feels he really must wear them, I suggest no socks. However, if he must wear them, they should be half-length rather than full-length, because the full-length ones tend to bunch up when one is trying to pull them over the ankles.

His slippers should be of the easily slipped-on-and-off variety.

It doesn't matter what style his briefs are. In fact, Y-fronts can provide some quite exciting effects.

For the woman, skirt and blouse or a button-through dress are more preferable to blouse and trousers, for the reason that women's trousers are nearly always tightish around the legs and are not easily removed.

It should not be necessary for her to wear stockings, if the room is properly heated, so that she can dispense with her girdle. Girdles have turned more strip-sessions into fiascos than any other garment. Think of the lovely sense of relaxed freedom after a day in a constricting girdle, and three or four hours without support won't harm those tummy muscles. If she feels she wants her legs covered, however, I suggest she wears tights. Quite a lot of fun can be had from the slow revelation of flesh as the tights are rolled down.

She, too, should wear cardigans rather than pullovers, to avoid messing up her hair. Nothing is more devastating to a hairdo than a garment pulled over the head, besides the difficulty that can be encountered trying to get it off.

She should be able to kick her slippers or shoes off easily.

Like the man, it doesn't matter what type of panties she wears. As for him, they are usually the last garment removed, and by that time the Sensuous Couple are so well away, that the traditional defiant gesture of the ecdyiast's art cannot fail to be exciting, even though it may sometimes be a little troublesome to perform.

Perhaps I have given the wrong impression in using

the term "strip-session." The Sensuous Man and the Sensuous Woman do not strip themselves off, they strip off one another.

Dressed as I have suggested, or at least along these lines, the Sensuous Couple sitting watching the TV after supper in a heavenly quiet house are ready at the whim of either to begin undressing as foreplay.

One Sensuous Couple I know signal the suggestion to one another by one clasping the other's hand and lightly tickling the palm with a finger-tip, a caress which is returned by the other to signify that he/she is on. But each couple can devise their own signal— a hand slipped inside a blouse or up a skirt, or placed over a breast outside the clothes and squeezing; a hand slipped inside a shirt and a nipple stroked, flicked, or lightly nipped or rolled, a hand placed over the crotch outside the trousers and squeezed a little. The Sensuous Couple will find a number of ingenious ways of letting each other know what they want.

They will also find variations on the theme which I am going to announce. I am limited by my personal experience, naturally, and though I like to think of myself as one-half of a Sensuous Couple, I am very conscious of the fact that there must be many Persons around who are far more Sensuous than I am. My scheme of things is what we found worked well for us. Other Sensuous Couples may think our way of doing things is feeble. Each to his own taste, and all that, but if I am going to say anything at all about the technique, then I must draw on my own experience. Though you may not think it, I am basically a modest sort of fellow, and I shall be much happier if I write in the Third (Sensuous) Person.

The first move, once the intention to strip has been

established, concentrates on the face and neck. Deep-kissing, nibbling ear lobes, flicking the tongue in the hollow behind the ear, kissing and tonguing the throat, eyelids and nose-tip (a very sensitive zone) are mutually administered.

(By the way, the secret of the Sensuous Couple's lovemaking is that they each work on the other simultaneously. There are, of course, one or two caresses which require positions in which the caresser is out of reach of the caressed; but this is, in my view, a "good thing", because it introduces variety, too. Variety is the spice of sex.)

At the same time hands are wandering. Various fastenings are unfastened while this reciprocal buccal caressing is in progress, e.g. the waist-band and fly-zip of the man's trousers, the buttons of his cardigan and shirt; the waist-band of her skirt or the buttons of her dress down to the waist, or of the cardigan or blouse.

After a few moments, the Sensuous Man's penis is bound to be stiff. Because of the constriction of trousers and briefs, especially if the briefs are close-fitting, it will not have been able to spring erect, but will be depressed downwards at an uncomfortable angle, if not a downright painful angle. The Sensuous Woman, therefore, slips her hand under the waist-band of the briefs, takes hold of the penis and pulls it up-right, so that it is lying along the pubic bone, nestling in the hair, its tip pointing towards the navel. Before withdrawing her hand, she gives it a friendly caress, a promise of treats to come.

Hands now come into play under shirt and blouse, while the two mouths continue their explorations and caressings. In a moment or two, the Sensuous Man will unclasp his partner's bra, which will then fall forward revealing the breasts. If, as my Sensuous Partner used to, the Sensuous Woman wears a strapless bra for evening homewear, it can be removed altogether by the Sensuous Man and nonchalantly tossed away. This means that besides applying hand, finger, lips and tongue-tip caresses to breasts and nipples, unimpeded, he can also carry out a pattern of tongue-tip caresses as far south as her navel. (If the bra cannot be removed completely because of its straps, it tends to get in the way of these manoeuvres.) While he is doing this, the Sensuous Woman will stroke his shoulders and back lightly with the palms of her hands.

A reminder: *It is essential that both partners are in mouth or hand contact with one another all the time,* except in the later stages, when one or two caress-manoeuvres place one body out of reach of the other's hands. In my experience, however, this need very, very rarely happen, for even if one partner is kneeling on the floor with the mouth engaged in the other's genital region, it usually is possible for the more passive partner to reach shoulders, nape and ears with his/her hands.

After some moments of mouth caresses of the Sensuous Woman's breasts, shoulders and belly by the Sensuous Man, they change roles. She now applies mouth caresses to his torso, while he strokes her shoulders and back.

By this time both will have developed what I term "tactile libido".

In all sessions of lovemaking in which Sensuous Couples are involved, there comes a moment when the Sensuous Man's penis becomes so swollen that it demands the direct attention of the hand or body. The same sort of desire is experienced, though to a rather less extent, by the Sensuous Woman in her vulval area (the area around the clitoris and vaginal entrance). It is in response to this urge that a couple will press their genital areas together with quite heavy pressure, from time to time; or the Sensuous Woman asks the Sensuous Man to press his knee into her crotch, or he lifts her knee right up behind his balls—taking care to move them out of the way so that they don't get squashed—and asking her to push up as hard as she can.

When the tactile libido comes into action when they are nude on the bed, or are engaged in the game our Sensuous Couple are presently playing, hands take the place of knees and other pressures. Each should give the other a sign. We used to say, "Touch me."

In response, the Sensuous Woman will slip her hand inside the waist-band of her Sensuous Partner's briefs, clasp his penis with the whole hand and squeeze it quite hard. The Sensuous Man will slip his hand inside the waist-band of his Sensuous Partner's panties, insert all four fingers into her crotch, and pull them upwards quite hard.

They should keep up these pressures for a minute or so, then withdraw the hands to use them elsewhere.

We always found it best to get the upper garments off first. The scarf or handkerchief, if he was wearing either, will have been removed from the Sensuous Man's neck while his Sensuous Partner was unbuttoning his shirt. Now she should slip his shirt and cardigan off in the same movement.

She doesn't drag them off, but slips them down over his shoulders slowly, leaning forward and tonguing his shoulders and neck as she does so. While she is doing this, he leans forward and kisses her breasts and plays with her nipples with his mouth. By leaning forward he makes it easier for her to slip off his shirt.

This is followed by another short session of mutual "tactile pressure" to keep both halves of the Couple happy.

Before the Sensuous Man begins to remove his Sensuous Partner's blouse and cardigan—together—they have a short session of mouth and hand caressing, which ends with the Sensuous Woman leaning forward and tonguing the Sensuous Man's nipples, torso and navel. While she is doing this, he slips off her blouse and cardigan by slow degrees, caressing the nape of her neck, shoulders and back as he does so.

Another short session of mutual tactile pressure comes after this, and runs into another round of caresses of naked torsos and backs.

We always found that it was easier if I stood up when we decided the rest of my clothes were to come off, while my Sensuous Partner sometimes knelt on a cushion on the floor or sometimes sat on the settee. If the Sensuous Couple decide to do this, the Sensuous Man can stand either back to or facing his partner.

As soon as he stands up, his trousers will fall about his feet. By this time he will more likely than not have kicked off his slippers, but if he has not done so, he will now. At the same time he should be able to step out of his trousers, but should he need assistance, his Sensuous Partner will help him, running her hands down the outsides of his legs to reach his trousers. He is wearing socks? As soon as he is free of his trousers he will lift each foot in turn so that she may remove them. They must come off now, because there is no more ludicrous sight than a man naked but for his pants and socks, or only his socks.

While helping him off with his trousers and/or socks, his Sensuous Partner will run her lips and tongue down his thighs.

She next slips both hands over his hips inside his briefs. By passing his hands down over his hips and thighs, she will draw down his briefs.

As soon as his penis and balls come into view, she will begin to smother them with kisses and other delectable caresses of tongue and mouth. Thus involved, she will draw the briefs right down to his ankles so that he can step out of them.

And there the Sensuous Man is in all his impeccable, rampant nudity!

If she kneels behind him, trousers and socks will be removed by her as just described. The briefs will be taken off in the same fashion, but more slowly, for as soon as his buttocks are exposed, she will cover them with kisses, while with one hand she reaches round and clasps and squeezes his penis and cradles his balls lightly in the other hand.

After a few moments of this, she swiftly removes his briefs altogether and then once more reaches round to penis and balls, while she brushes her breasts lightly, oh, so lightly! against his buttocks and thighs.

This is one of the most crazy-making caresses of the strip-technique repertoire. Don't use it before this stage of the strip is reached because you need the preceding gradual build-up to bring you up to the state in which you can fully appreciate, both of you, the subtlety of the gossamer kiss of those extra-sensory tips of her stone-hard clamant nipples.

Whatever the Sensuous Woman has been wearing, more likely than not it will have fallen about her feet and she will have stepped out of it during her final ministrations to her Sensuous Partner. If this has happened or not, we found it more convenient if she stood facing the standing Sensuous Man, because even if she has only her panties between him and her nudity, most types of panties tend to be clinging and are not so amenable to removing hands as are a man's briefs.

Working on her torso, beginning at her shoulders, with hands and mouth semi-frenzied to caress, the Sensuous Man gradually slips his hands down to the waist-band of her panties. Their arrival there unfailingly causes whatever other covering that may still be clinging to her to drop.

Passing his hands down over her buttocks, he forces the panties down with them. While he is doing so, his mouth is doing all it knows to send ripples of sensations from breasts to loins. As his hands force the panties down over her thighs, he goes slowly down on one knee, but never loses mouth or tongue contact with her belly as he does so.

Almost invariably he will find that he has to push the panties right down to her ankles, and she will have to lift her feet one by one to step out of them. This action will slightly open her genital lips. By a strange chance, his mouth will be exactly opposite them at this moment. Out darts his tongue, and with lightning flicks of its tip he greets her miniscule penis as it protrudes haughtily from its hood.

The action of the tongue creates a new wave of need for tactile pressure. She places her hands on the back of his head and crushes his mouth hard against her. At the same time he seizes her buttocks with both hands and kneads them firmly. It is quite likely that in the next moment or two she will have her first grand climax.

As a variation, my Sensuous Partner used sometimes to stand with her back to me. While my hands played on her breasts, my mouth would play on her shoulders and back. Then I would slip my hands down over her belly, pausing for a moment at her navel, then work their way under the waist-band of her panties and down over her thighs.

When I was down on my knees, I would smother her buttocks with kisses, or snake my tongue back and forth across them in flickering darts. Free of all her clothes at last, I would slide my hands back up the insides of her legs and thighs, until, reaching her crotch, I would insert three fingers between her genital lips and, placing the other hand over the assaulting hand, press on her hard. Behind her, my face would press in the opposite direction. Every time, within seconds, she would come.

The Sensuous Couple have now a number of alternatives before them:

1. Hurry immediately to the bedroom and finish off on the bed;

   (a) in a frenzy of urgency;

   (b) take up where they left off and come to a leisurely climax or two.

2. Continue for a time on the settee, which lends itself well to a number of caresses which are not so comfortably executed on the bed, e.g. perineal caresses by either partner. (The perineum, by the way, is the ridge between anus and vagina/anus and high up behind the balls.) It is a very sensitive zone indeed,

yet quite a number of Sensuous Couples overlook it.
In both the Sensuous Man and the Sensuous Woman
it is highly susceptible to light caresses of a finger
tip, or to heavy pressure at mid-point—some very
Sensuous Men can be brought off by this pressure
alone and no other attention—but it is most susceptible to the stroking of the tongue-tip.

This tongue-tip stroking is worth knowing about.
The Sensuous Woman lies on her back on the settee,
her head on cushions, her buttocks tilted up on one
of the arms, her knees bent and either drawn right up
to her breasts, or just so far that her feet are resting
on the settee arm. Her legs are parted. The Sensuous
Man stands—or, if he is tall, kneels on a pouffe or
footstool, at the end of the settee, and beginning at
the anus he runs the tip of the tongue up the length
of the perineum to the vagina-entrance. He circles the
vaginal rim for a second or two, flicks his tongue in
and out of the vagina a few times, continues up the
vaginal ridge to the clitoris, pauses there for a few
more seconds, with the tongue movement his Sensuous Partner prefers. He then begins to bring his
tongue back the way it has come, pauses at the
vagina-entrance, then very slowly progresses down the
perineum, in two-strides-forward-one-back action until
he comes to the anus, which he touches only if the
woman is sensitive there. This caress is repeated as
many times as the Sensuous Woman can stand, or
until she wants a change.

The Sensuous Man takes up the same position on
the settee as the Sensuous Woman did. She stands at
the end of the settee, and beginning at his anus, she
strokes his perineum with her tongue-tip. When she
comes to his balls, she passes the flat of her tongue

over them, and continues up the shaft of his penis in the same fashion until she reaches his frenum. There she reverts to tongue-tip and teases the frenum and penis-tip with it for a few moments, before she begins the return journey. Repeat by desire.

It will be appreciated that it is very difficult for the stroked partner to reach any part of the other's body in this position, and on further consideration it will be seen how difficult it would be to tilt up the bottom sufficiently to expose the anus, if the caress were carried out on the bed.

After a session of foreplay on the settee, the Sensuous Couple can, if they wish, transfer themselves to the bedroom, where they can either begin a new and different session of foreplay, or carry on where they left off.

3. Work out the whole session on the settee.

4. Go to the kitchen and have some refreshment, and then finish off the session there.

The alternatives are really dependent on the ingenuity of the Sensuous Couple. One thing, however, I can assure you—undressing as foreplay skilfully and imaginatively executed invariably raises tension to such a pitch that even breaking off to go upstairs or make a drink in the kitchen does not impair it much, and it is very easy indeed to get back to where you were when you broke off. Apart from this, however, used as an "occasional technique" it is guaranteed to turn any Sensuous Couple on like nobody's business.

If it is new to you, try it and see!

CHAPTER SEVEN

AROUSAL ABLUTIONS

I don't know whether you are aware of it, but there is something of a controversy going on, on both sides of the Atlantic, about the use of sex-deodorants, which have recently become something of a rage in America, and are beginning to take on over here.

There is a school of experts who maintain that sex odours, among which sweat is included, are quite powerful stimulators of Sensuous Men and Sensuous Women *once they have been turned on.* I cannot speak for others, but while sweat does have a sexually exhilarating effect on me. I don't go crazy about other odours, possibly because my sense of smell isn't all that great, so that they are too subtle for me. But I have met men who agree that they are stimulated by genital odours, and women who have found the distinctive musky smell the penis of some men gives off after some minutes of arousal very exciting. On the other hand, I've met just as many Sensuous Men and Sensuous Women who have reacted violently against the suggestion that sex-odours are aphrodisiacs.

But whatever the rights and wrongs of the argument, I am all for both sexes washing genital areas and anuses thoroughly before beginning a session of lovemaking. This isn't to remove smells—though I don't care what anyone says, unless you are a urolagnist you will not find the smell of stale urine which adheres to the pubic hair of even the most fastidiously clean woman, unless she washes, arousing—but to cut down on the possible germ-intake during oral intercourse. The man has a special duty to wash his penis well on this account, especially if he is not circumcised, for the penis, and especially a hooded one, is a natural meeting-place for dust, grit and germs collected from clothing.

This is something I feel very strongly about, and I would like to point out to the pro-sex-odours enthusiasts that washing will not spoil their fun, because the odours only have their effect *after* full arousal has taken place, by which time the secretions which supply the odours will have re-established themselves. In other words, no amount of preliminary washing can do them out of their special form of enjoyment.

It is my firm conviction that all Sensuous Couples should perform genital ablutions *three* times a day as a matter of routine:

1. On getting up—so as to start the day fresh:
2. The Sensuous Man when he changes for the evening, and the Sensuous Woman, if she changed earlier, just before supper, to be prepared for a possible strip-session:
3. Immediately before going to bed, if they haven't had a strip session.

It is this third ablution I am interested in here.

The Sensuous Couple, as I have said before, never miss a trick, and they don't miss this one. They turn the ablution routine into an arousal technique on those nights when it is quite apparent that before they fall asleep, they are going to make love.

It is on account of Arousal Ablutions that I insisted in Chapter 2 that there should be facilities of one sort or another in the bedroom. (That foxed you, didn't it? You thought I was thinking about washing down after intercourse. Perish the thought! All you want to do then is cuddle up gratefully and lovingly to one another; not get out of bed and destroy the effects of all the good work by sluicing down. You won't catch a dreadful disease if you postpone it until the morning.)

As with almost every other technique the Sensuous Couple go in for, the Arousal Ablution Technique is performed by the Sensuous Man and the Sensuous Woman and Vice-Versa—simultaneously.

Fill the basin with warm water. Two pieces of soap have been laid out, and each takes one and drops it into the water. Moisten the hand that is going to operate well with water, and with it moisten the genital regions of the Sensuous Partner.

Next remove the soap from the water and apply it to the genital regions of each liberally. Put down the soap and replace the hand on the soaped parts.

The hand now wanders, leaving no crook or cranny unexplored, from anus to clitoris, from penis-head to anus.

The soap has already, by its slipperiness, added to the tactile sensitivity of the already responsive parts that are under attention. I needn't detail the manoeuvres of those hands for the Sensuous Couple—pumping the penis, teasing the clitoris, lathery fondling of balls, exploratory fingers in vagina, and mutual caresses of anus.

If the penis of the Sensuous Man isn't at least half-erect and the genital lips of the Sensuous Woman aren't swollen and ready for tacitly promised further attentions by the time the moment to sluice off the soap and dry off, they have forfeited the right to the title Sensuous Couple.

But the preparations don't end there!

No self-respecting woman retires for the night with the pores of her facial skin clogged with cream, rouge and powder. She takes off her face, and has her own personal routine for doing so.

Once the Sensuous Man and the Sensuous Woman have decided to become a Sensuous Couple, she must teach him her special routine for taking off her face without delay.

The Arousal Ablutions complete, she will sit on her vanitory stool and he will sit opposite her on the stool which they use for one of the variations of the woman-astride-sitting positions. With one hand he will cream her face and do whatever else she does, slowly and carefully, and with the other he will caress her other pouting lips, not forgetting to give her a foretaste of delights to come with a finger or two in the vagina; and if she, at the same time, caresses his balls and penis with one hand, and plays with a nipple with the other, by the time they are ready to roll on to the bed they will be ready for anything.

Arousal Ablutions should always be a part of foreplay when the Sensuous Couple embark on an afternoon session, though then the taking off of the Sensuous Woman's face may be omitted.

Ingenuity pays dividends in this technique. I have only made a few suggestions.

CHAPTER EIGHT

THE PENIS AS STIMULATOR

I am being constantly astonished—and astonished is not too strong a word—by the number of people who overlook the penis itself as a stimulator in foreplay. Mind you, to use it in this way does call for absolute Orgasm-Control on the part of the Sensuous Man, but the Sensuous Man has not the right to the title unless he has absolute Orgasm-Control. The fact that a large number of Sensuous Men have never heard of the "penis as stimulator", adds to my mystification, because the Sensuous Man must also be the Sexually Imaginative Man.

However, don't let's waste time trying to unravel the mystery. Let me instead put down a number of ways in which I use the penis, from time to time, to caress some sensitive spot or other on the Sensitive Partner.

THE CLITORIS

The first of these spots is the obvious one—the clitoris and vaginal ridge. There are a number of ways in which this little key to the Sensuous Woman's whole sexual responsiveness can be reached.

(a) The Sensuous Couple lie on their sides facing one another and the Sensuous Man, holding his penis just below the rim, with two fingers on the frenum and the thumb on top, teases the clitoris, which the Sensuous Woman is exposing for him by holding the lips apart, with the always softly supple slippery penis-head.

Apparently, the effect of this caress of the clitoris is quite different in quality from the caress by a finger, or even by the tongue. I have never been able to experience it myself, so I cannot confirm or dispute it; but I would like to suggest that a lot of the effect is in the mind sparked off by the idea that in this caress the Two Greatest Lovers come into direct contact.

But why look for a reason? No Sensuous Couple want to make love only for reasons.

(b) The Sensuous Man lies on top of the Sensuous Woman, who with her fingers keeps her lips parted and the clitoris exposed. He places his penis along the vaginal ridge with the head in the hair just above the clitoris, so that when he raises his buttocks a little the penis-head comes down over it, and when he lowers them, returns so that raising and lowering of the buttocks moves the penis backwards and forwards across the clitoris. If the buttocks swing rhythmically, again Sensuous Partners using the technique have claimed that the sensations are superb.

I can personally testify that one Sensuous Man, at any rate, gets an especial kick out of this one, because his penis-head is very responsive to being caressed by hair. Many other Sensuous Men he knows admit to similar experiences.

(c) The Sensuous Man again lies on top of the Sensuous Woman, but slightly higher up her, so that the base of his penis, about an inch above the root, makes contact with the clitoris. He presses quite hard on the clitoris and moves his penis backwards and forwards on it by buttock-swinging.

(d) The Sensuous Man kneels astride the Sensuous Woman with his back to her, his bottom resting lightly on her belly, and himself placed in such a position that when he parts her lips to expose her clitoris with one hand and depresses his penis with the other, the penis-head makes contact with the clitoris. He rolls his penis-head from side to side over the clitoris with the fingers holding it down.

By the way, only two fingers hold back the lips, in a "wish-bone" attitude, and the penis-head is inserted between the fingers.

This is generally a technique for older men, over the age, say, of forty. Younger men's erections tend to be much more upstanding than the older man's, and to depress the penis this far would hurt. It seems that as time passes, practice makes the penis much more versatile in its movement-capacity; but in any case, the angle of the older erect penis, while losing nothing at all of its stiffness, takes up a stance that is more horizontal than not.

Still, this shouldn't stop a younger man from trying it out if he wants to. Who knows, it might not hurt him at all.

THE VAGINAL MUSCLE

Only the first third of the length of the vaginal barrel has any sensitivity, and of this portion the muscle surrounding the entrance is most sensitive.

The Sensuous Man lies on top of his Sensuous

Partner and puts only the head of his penis as far as the rim, in the vagina.

By buttock-swinging he teases the rim of the vaginal muscle with the rim of his penis-head.

Most Sensuous Women are turned on really high by this and make their appreciation known vocally, even when normally they are not erolalists.

THE BREASTS

You will remember the story of the Sensuous Woman I related earlier on, who liked her Sensuous Partner to stimulate a nipple with his penis-tip until he came, and then came herself as his semen engulfed her nipple?

Well, lots of Sensuous Women, though not taking it to this particular conclusion, admit to being turned on by nipple-penis contact, so it's worth a try.

THE ARM-PITS

Most men and women are moderately, and quite a lot highly, sensitive in the arm-pits.

The Sensuous Woman sits or kneels on the bed or on an armless chair, with her back to her Sensuous Partner, who places himself behind her, standing, and puts his penis under her arm, high up in the pit. She lowers her arm to her side so that the penis is lightly held just in contact with the arm and trunk by it.

The man swings with his buttocks, just as he does when he has his penis in the vagina. If he leans forward a little he can see the penis-head appearing and disappearing at the top of the woman's breast, which he finds visually stimulating.

As well as being stimulated by the movement of the penis in the arm-pit, many Sensuous Women are also visually stimulated by watching the penis-head bobbing in and out by their breasts, one of the few visual stimuli that affects quite a number of women.

I am personally much more stimulated if my Sensuous Partner has not shaved under the arms; but as most of them do, I haven't often had this pleasanter experience. However, the sensations I do get are more than worthwhile; I am not complaining; and I don't think any other Sensuous Man will who tries it.

THE CROOK OF THE KNEE

Most Sensuous Women, and a large number of Sensuous Men, are highly sensitive to light caresses of the palm of the hand, the mouth and tongue in the area at the back of the knee. This area is also sensitive to movements of the penis.

The Sensuous Woman sits on the bed or settee, with one or both knees drawn up. The Sensuous Man stands at her side, and inserts his penis in the crook of the knee—if she keeps her knees together and he can produce 7 inches or more, he can usually reach the further knee-crook as well, and so double the sensations for the woman—and swings his buttocks as he does when he has his penis in the vagina.

By the way, the degree to which the knee is bent must be nicely adjusted. It must not be bent so much that the penis is gripped by it and can hardly be moved; and not enough so that the penis does not make maximum contact with the skin of the knee-crook while moving freely.

These are just a few tips for using the penis as stimulator. No doubt the really ingenious Sensuous Couple will find other methods.

CHAPTER NINE

THE ART OF THE BATH AND THE SHOWER

No Sensuous Couple can claim to have a full repertoire of sex techniques unless they make full use of the bath and the shower.

In Chapter 2, I made some recommendations about the size of the bath and the type of shower, and all I want to do now is to offer a few hints about techniques which I believe will help to make the most of these aquatic sessions.

Many Sensuous Couples find that the deliberate intent to couple in the bath so mentally stimulates them that they do not need a long session of preliminary foreplay. Others, however, claim that the grand climax in the bath is always more thrilling if they have one of their usual sessions of foreplay, and then transfer to the bathroom.

While waiting for the bath to run, they can carry on with their caresses so that the build-up of excitement does not fall completely back. I can recommend a combination of mutual caresses which includes the Arousal Ablution Technique.

It often escapes even Sensuous People that the toes, especially the great toes, can be sensitive to stroking with the fingers lightly or to light sucking. (Attention to the feet is as essential as it is to the genital area if the latter technique is ever used; but the toe-nails should be kept in good trim all the time, as you will see presently.)

The bath-session should begin with the Sensuous Man, always the height of politeness to his Sensuous Partner, getting into the bath at the tap-end, while she enters at the other end. The first three or four minutes they spend stimulating each other with their great toes. He finds and caresses her clitoris with the ball of his toe, while she seeks out his perineum and stimulates it with the nail side of hers.

It is NOT recommended, however beautifully trimmed he keeps his toe-nails, that he should try to penetrate his Sensuous Partner's vagina with his toe.

Nearly all Sensuous Couples with whom I have discussed the toe-caress technique say that because they use it fairly infrequently they are completely turned on by it and are ready for coupling in a comparatively short time.

There are two ways in which they can couple. One, facing one another as they are, they move towards one another until the Sensuous Woman is sitting on the Sensuous Man's lap impaled on his penis. He stimulates her clitoris with a finger, and she contracts and relaxes her vaginal muscle on his penis. While doing this, by gently rocking backwards and forwards, they bring each other to climax. Two, they change places, and the man, supporting his head, shoulder-blades and the base of his spine on the foam cushions I recommended in Chapter 2, lies as straight as he can. The

Sensuous Woman either straddles him, facing him, or lies on him on her back. While he caresses her clitoris with a finger, and a nipple with his other hand, she caresses his penis with her vagina by raising and lowering her buttocks *slightly* and rather slowly, so that the water is not sent splashing over the sides of the bath onto the floor. So they come to their grand climax. By the way, if she can reach down and fondle his balls, he will be in the Seventh Heaven of Sensuousness.

Everyone who uses the bath for lovemaking, myself among them, testifies that the sensations built up, the petit climaxes and the grand climaxes, have a quality about them which it is not possible to capture in any other kind of lovemaking. In my view, this is because the warm water is continually moving and has a very subtle caressing action on the vital sensitive spots which no other form of caressing can imitate.

The Technique of the Shower works on quite the opposite principle.

It is a useful technique for concluding a session in which the foreplay has been unusually active and the Sensuous Couple is iridescent with sweat. When they get under the shower—together—they have the spray operating and they soap one another all over, incorporating the Arousal Ablution Technique.

When they are ready to join up, they can do so, either facing or by rear-entry. The Sensuous Man adjusts the shower from spray to jet. If they are facing, they hold on to one another by the arms, and lean their torsos away from one another in such a way that the fierce jet of water is directed on to the Sensuous Woman's clitoris and the top-side of the base of the Sensuous Man's penis. Quite a number of couples find the action of the jet on both these spots sufficient to bring them both to climax without any movement except vaginal-rim contractions by the woman, or the slightest of buttock movements.

In the rear-entry position, the Sensuous Woman leans forward, and after insertion the Sensuous Man leans back, with the base of his penis exposed so that the jet of water can be directed on to them both. Usually he will have to make buttock swings while the Sensuous Woman may have to caress her clitoris, until they both reach the point-of-no-return, which they will time to do simultaneously.

At the first orgasmic flush they stay perfectly still and let the jet of water on their bodies rush them to the grand climax.

Properly developed, both the Bath and the Shower Technique can add a new dimension to the Sensuous Couple's sex experience.

If you haven't tried them, don't lose too much time. You may find you will need some practice to get them perfect, but, honestly, the time spent on them will not be wasted.

CHAPTER TEN

THE TECHNIQUES OF ORAL INTERCOURSE

The Sensuous Couple know all about oral intercourse, and having no hang-ups about its being filthy, sinful, shameful, disgusting, degrading and a hundred and one other arguments against it that non-sensuous people put up, they make it a prominent part of their lovemaking techniques. They would be stupid not to, because the mouth and the tongue, besides being sensitive zones in themselves have special qualities as stimulating agents that no other organ or limb has.

Because the mouth and the tongue have these dual functions, oral love is a two-way traffic. While stimulating the Sensuous Partner's clitoris, vagina or penis, by doing so the stimulator is arousing himself/herself.

Besides being a technique, it is also an art, and one which is not always easy to acquire, even by Sensuous Men and Sensuous Women. So far I have not seen advice offered to the would-be Sensuous Person which is all that helpful. It's all very well to talk about Cream Whirls, Butterfly Flickers and other exotic activities, if the aim is not clearly defined and the path to its achievement well laid out, not necessarily in complete detail, but nevertheless clear enough for anyone to get the message, what's the use? I know I am being arrogant, but I would like to put in a word or two on the subject myself.

The aim of oral intercourse is to turn the Sensuous Partner wildly on, only even more so, and to be turned on oneself at the same time. Mouth and tongue, clitoris and vagina, and penis, constitute the path. The reciprocal caresses—of tongue and clitoris, clitoris and tongue, of mouth plus tongue and vagina, vagina and tongue plus mouth, of mouth plus tongue and penis, penis and tongue plus mouth—bring the two bodies together in a fusion of sensations equalled only by the coupling of penis and vagina.

In case there are would-be Sensuous Couples reading this who are not already acquainted with the concept of oral intercourse, and are puzzled by my references to mouth and tongue caressing clitoris, vagina and penis, and being caressed by them, let me say briefly what is involved.

When the Sensuous Man orally stimulates the clitoris and vagina of his Sensuous Partner it is called *cunnilingus*. Cunnilingus involves sucking the clitoris with the lips, licking or flicking it with the tongue or tongue-tip, licking the vaginal ridge, sucking the genital-lips with the mouth-lips and inserting the tongue in the vagina.

When the Sensuous Woman orally stimulates the penis of her Sensuous Partner it is called *fellatio*, and she is said to be fellating him. Fellatio involves licking and flicking the penis-head and shaft with the tongue and tongue-tip, and taking the penis into the mouth and sucking it.

I know *cunnilingus* and *fellatio* are stilted, artificial terms. I don't like them one little bit, but they are useful to have in one's vocabulary, because they are a kind of shorthand, since each requires several words to describe it. There are various vernacular phrases for them but the trouble with these phrases is that they are bi-sexual. Cunnilingus and fellatio are heterosexual, and you do know where you are with them—cunnilingus is what a *man* does to a woman, fellatio is what a *woman* does to a man.

When one says, "The woman licks the man's penis and takes it into her mouth and sucks it," and "The man sucks and licks the woman's clitoris," it sounds simple enough, doesn't it? But actually fellatio and cunnilingus are quite sophisticated techniques.

Taking fellatio first, let me try to give the basic outlines of the techniques.

Fellatio is not just a matter of putting the penis-head in the mouth and sucking it. Naturally, this simple activity would give the man a good deal of pleasure, but as with every other stimulating technique, the aim is to give him the maximum pleasure. To provide him with the maximum pleasure, the fellator must know the sensitive areas of the penis. These are—in descending order of sensitivity—the frenum, penis-tip, rim (both round the edge and in the groove under it), the base of the penis all round about an inch and a half above the root, the whole length of the underside of the shaft, and finally, the rest of the skin of the penis.

Since the frenum, penis-head and rim lead off the list with maximum sensitivity, if the man is uncircumcised it is essential to draw back his foreskin as far as it will go before beginning fellatio, otherwise some of the effect will be lost, because the mouth and tongue cannot be in direct contact with the extensive masses of nerves in these three closely located areas. Also the warmth of the mouth and the saliva it contains are extremely stimulating in their special way.

One thing about fellatio a woman must never forget. The head of the erect penis is extremely sensitive and she must take particular care all the time not to bite or scratch it with her teeth. Should she do so, she can be absolutely certain of disaster. Nothing makes the penis more rapidly deflate than pain. A sharp nip, and within two seconds it will be completely limp, and will take a great deal of the friendliest persuasion to get it back up again.

So the first technique of fellatio the Sensuous Woman must learn, as "J" so rightly pointed out in *The Sensuous Woman*, is to draw her lips down and under (or over) the edges of her teeth to shield her delicate target from their sharpness. She should not draw them in so much that they are completely rigid, but just enough to cover them.

In my humble opinion, the position in which you get yourself to perform fellatio is important. Many Sensuous Men find being fellated standing up very exciting, and to do so the woman nearly always kneels on the floor. If she does adopt this position, the Sensuous Woman will first have provided herself with cushions to kneel on, and so avoid a good deal of discomfort. It is a good position because the frenum is directly available to her tongue and so is the underside of the penis. Besides, unless the man is very tall, she will not have to depress the penis very much when she takes it into her mouth.

Some Sensuous Men find this standing position too exciting, especially if they are fellated until they come. The rising excitement can make the knees quiver uncontrollably, and the shaking can be so violent that he has difficulty in keeping his balance. Trying to do so can kill half the sensations. These men usually prefer to sit down, with the woman kneeling between their knees—on cushions.

If fellatio is used only as a foreplay technique, and the session is going to end with the penis in the vagina, then I suggest that the Sensuous Couple should lie on the bed. The Sensuous Woman should have her face towards his face, and her bottom towards his feet, rather than the other way round, because once again, the frenum is directly presented to her tongue, which does not happen if she has her bottom towards his face.

What must be taken into consideration is the

strength of the Sensuous Man's erection, which, as I have already pointed out twice, will vary according to his age. A man between 16 and 40 can have an erection that is so strong that the penis stalks upright, its head nodding against his belly when he stands. When the erection is this strong, more than a few degrees of depression can be quite painful, and this is why the fellating partner's approach to it is so important. One way or another, she must take up such a position that her tongue and lips are within reach of the frenum and penis-tip without the whole of the penis having to be depressed too much.

After a man reached the age of thirty-five to forty, though his erection is as strong as ever, it is possible to depress the penis through at least forty-five degrees, without causing him any pain. Usually the penis can be brought up to stand at right angles with the rest of his body when he is on his back, without causing him any discomfort whatsoever. Having this knowledge at her fingertips—and it is so important that I do not apologise for repeating it—the sensible Sensuous Woman will adjust her fellatio position accordingly.

Most Sensuous Couples agree that simultaneous oral caresses are exciting only just short of the excitement which the penis in the vagina gives rise to. In order to carry out this simultaneous stimulation, one or other variations of the position known as "69" must be used.

One variant is for the couple to lie side by side with their mouths within easy reach of each other's genitals. It is a restful position, but it has the drawback that the man is not very well placed to caress the clitoris and vagina. It's a bit difficult to explain why this is, but try it and you will see what I mean.

By far the most satisfactory "69" position is when
the man lies on his back and the woman crouches
astride and above him. Her clitoris and vagina are
then directly over his face and her own mouth is within easy reach of his penis. If she lets it lie flat on his
belly she can tongue his frenum and the underside of
his penis, and when she wants to take it into her
mouth, she can lift it up just sufficiently to get it into
her mouth, or, if a greater angle is not painful, so high
that she can milk it directly from above.

Whether oral caresses are going to be used as foreplay or as an alternative to penis-vagina contact, i.e.
continued to orgasm, before taking the penis into her
mouth, the Sensuous Woman gives the frenum, penis-
head and rim a warming-up by licking them, or teasing them with rapidly moving tongue-tip. This can be
followed by a number of varieties of caresses, as, for
example, running the tongue round the edge of the
rim, the tongue-tip under the edge of the rim, licking
the frenum and penis-tip with the tongue, and *very,
very lightly* nipping or rolling the frenum between lip-
protected teeth. Blowing on the penis-head and under
the rim is also extremely stimulating.

When the Sensuous Woman eventually takes the
penis into her mouth, she should take as much in as
she can without retching. Simultaneously with her
sucking of the penis, she must move her mouth up and
down the shaft and head. Most Sensuous Men like to
control these movements, so if her Sensuous Partner
puts his hands on her head to do this, she should follow the rhythm of his hands.

Since the penis must be held away from his belly,
in order for this manoeuvre to be carried out, the Sensuous Woman should move the hand holding it up and

down that part of the penis which will not go into her mouth. With the other hand she should fondle his balls—again very, very lightly. If his balls are not too large, she should take one or both into her mouth from time to time and suck them gently. Most Sensuous Men find this extremely arousing, but good care must be taken not to nip them with the teeth or suck on them too hard.

As the Sensuous Man's arousal sensations begin to build up, the Sensuous Woman will notice that his balls now and again move up towards the root of his penis, pause there for a second or two, and then move down again. When he is approaching the point-of-no-return, he will begin to breathe heavily, and will automatically push up and lower his pelvis rhythmically.

At the same time his balls will rise and lower more frequently, and they will not now descend so low as they did previously.

When this begins to happen the Sensuous Woman will know that he is going to climax within 30 to 60 seconds.

The really Sensuous Woman will have no compunction about letting him ejaculate in her mouth. I am quite convinced that if it were not for the pulsating of the penis as it squirts out the semen, most women would be unaware that her partner was ejaculating into her mouth. However, I must concede that some men's semen has a distinctly acid taste which very slightly stings the back of the throat as it is swallowed.

If the Sensuous Woman is not keen, for this or any other reason, to accept the semen in her mouth, as soon as his balls begin to get agitated she can withdraw her mouth and finish him off with her fingers. However, if she does this she must deprive him of some of his thrill, and to my way of thinking cannot claim to be a truly Sensuous Woman. If the semen tastes at all, it is not a strong taste, and a drink of water—or champagne—will immediately dispel any slight stinging sensations there may be. Certainly, swallowing semen never did any woman any harm. It can't, because for the most part it is made up of salts and vitamins.

The art of cunnilingus is just as subtle. If it is not to be performed simultaneously with fellatio, the woman should lie on her back, her knees drawn up and spread, the soles of her feet resting on the bed. The Sensuous Man places himself below her, his face over her genitals and his hands parting her genital lips.

He begins by running round the rim of her vaginal entrance with his tongue-tip, from time to time putting his tongue into her vagina as far as it will go, and moving it in and out, in the same way that his penis would if it were there. After a few minutes he runs the flat of his tongue up the vaginal ridge until he reaches the clitoris.

Having got there, he varies his caresses between:

(a) Licking the clitoris slowly with the flat of his tongue;

(b) Teasing the clitoris-head with rapid flicks of the tongue-tip;

(c) Taking the clitoris-head between his lips and sucking strongly on it;

(d) Rolling the clitoris-head between his lips;

(e) Any other technique he may invent himself.

The secret is to devote, say, a couple of minutes or three to direct stimulation of the clitoris by one or a combination of these methods, then return to the vagina for a moment or two and then come back to the clitoris.

When the woman comes up to the point-of-no-return she will begin to breathe heavily and the Sensuous Man will lose contact with the clitoris, because at this point the little darling Bud of May draws back into its hood. He is now faced with two alternatives; either he can apply a strong suction on her clitoral area, which will climax her within a few seconds, or rapidly pull himself up on to her, slip his penis into her vagina, and with a dozen thrusts or so, climax her that way, and himself as well.

All these manoeuvres, except the last, can be carried out in the "69" position I most warmly recommend, in which the woman crouches over the supine man.

The Sensuous Couple, who occasionally want to climax with simultaneous cunnilingus and fellatio, should be able, with a little practice to time their climaxes to coincide. And believe me, it is quite an experience! It is the only type of simultaneously achieved orgasm that I will go for.

Either as foreplay or as complete intercourse, oral lovemaking is never a disappointment, and, more often than not, provides a truly wild and deeply satisfying session.

If I were asked: Supposing you were allowed to use one type of caress, and only one, which would you choose? I would have no hesitation, even for a single second, in replying, "The mutual oral kind."

And I am quite sure that every Sensuous Couple would agree with me.

CHAPTER ELEVEN

EROLALIA

I cannot imagine a session of lovemaking in which neither partner speaks or makes any kind of appreciative sound. I am well aware that quite a number of men and women make love in complete silence, but I am also certain such people will never qualify as Sensuous Men and Sensuous Women.

There are a number of us, and I am one of them, who are automatically "noisy lovers". We just can't help ourselves; try as we may to stifle our appreciative words or noises when a particularly sensitive spot is given a particularly effective caress. When we are in the throes of climaxing we are at our most noisy, and it was when one of my partners once protested that the neighbours in all the rest of the apartments would hear me if I didn't control myself, that I discovered, I think, why we do it, which, in turn, decided me to recommend erolalia to those who do not naturally use the technique.

I tried to control my vocalising, because I didn't want to appear ungentlemanly to my partner. But when I did, I found that I had to hold my breath and that this made me self-conscious. When I tried soundless orgasm, the whole of my body went rigid and taut and the orgasm-sensations themselves were so much

97

less intense that they were hardly worth the effort.

The next opportunity I had of really letting myself go, I noticed that vocalising completely relaxed me, making the build-up of sensations more easily achieved and very much more intense in quality. I happened, on this occasion, to be with a partner who had never made love with an erolalist before.

"Do you always make such a din?" she asked, after we had both got back our breaths.

"I'm afraid so," I said, thinking to myself, here comes the 'what will the neighbours think' gambit again.

So I was a bit surprised when she said instead, "I found it terribly exciting."

"You did?" I said. She lived in Kensington, by the way.

"Yes. Whenever you made a little noise when I did some particular thing to you, it made me feel terribly good. I thought, 'I must be really doing my stuff today,' and I wanted to do even better. The more you let me know how much you were really enjoying what I was doing to you, the more randy I felt myself becoming. Then when you really let rip as you climaxed, I swear it made *me* climax ever so much more wildly, and afterwards I felt so good, because I had done this to you."

I told her that she could be right, because I found whenever I made love with a partner who was also a bit on the noisy side, my own build-up seemed much more intense. I also told her that I got all uptight if I couldn't vocalise, and I suggested she should try it, and see if it had any effect on her.

She was a little self-conscious about doing it at first, but she soon got the hang of it. She enthusiastically assured me that I was really right; she had never come so terribly wildly before; and she was quite mad not having known about it until now.

After that I discussed it with a number of friends, some of whom were already erolalists. They agreed with me. If ever, for some reason or other, they had to keep their erolalia in check, the session was never half so good. Some of those who had not heard of it before, tried it, and were amazed at the difference it made.

As Alice and Jim discovered, it not only works for the couple who do it, it is also stimulating for the couple who overhear it. If you do it and are able to overhear it at the same time, its effectiveness is even greater.

Besides the release of physical tensions which relaxes the muscles and other organs involved in love-making, which in turn makes the sensations much more acute, there is a sound psychological reason for it being partner-stimulating as well as self-stimulating.

As I have said so many times before, we make love to one another because we want to show the partner how emotionally involved we are with him/her; just how deeply emotionally involved we try to get across by making the session as intensely stimulating and sexually satisfying physically as we can by our foreplay techniques.

As my little friend so wisely pointed out after she had done it once or twice, "It makes terrible sense, doesn't it? How can one know if one is really pleasing someone unless they let one know how appreciative they are?"

She was wise in her generation, that one! When a couple make love in complete silence you can only take it for granted that everything is going O.K. because they are not complaining that they are not.

If we are told how good we are being—not in so many words, but with the hiss of indrawn breath, long-drawn-out "Ahs" and "Ohs", pantings, whimpers, groans, moans, and any suitable comments that come into our heads—we have pride enough in ourselves to make us want to do even better.

What's more, we do better; and we feel good because our partner feels good.

I ran into a young friend one evening, and noticed he was looking extremely pleased with himself.

"Won the pools?" I asked.

"Nothing so vulgar as that," he grinned.

"What then?"

"I've just made love for the first time with a girl I used to think wasn't very interested in sex."

"So?"

"Everything I did to her, she kept whispering, 'It's fantastic!' When we got really down to it she bucked to the rhythm of the word, saying it more and more quickly, the quicker we went. And before I got off her, she kept saying, 'You're fantastic!' and I got the feeling that I really must be, though no one else has told me so before. Anyhow, it's made me feel really good."

I am so convinced of the rightness and truth of what I have been saying, that in my book no couple can legitimately claim to be a truly Sensuous Couple unless they let one another know, in unmistakable terms, how much they appreciate one another; and not just afterwards, but during.

Erolalia is not a technique that can be taught. The Sensuous Couple will discover quickly enough how to express themselves and how they feel. Like all their other techniques, this, too, can be constantly improved.

If you are not already erolalia afficionados, do try it out!

CHAPTER TWELVE

AL FRESCO SEX

I have probably given the impression by what I said earlier on that because I condemn lovemaking in the back of a motor, in a pine forest or a hay meadow, that I am against all *al fresco* sex.

Not at all! What I am against is trying to make love in places that by their very nature must carry risks, and heavy risks at that, of something happening which will make the session a physically uncomfortable one, and one which will end up in fiasco. Comfort and security are so essential to any lovemaking couple— because of the powerful influence the mind has over how we function physically—that I would rather forego lovemaking than run the risk of this happening.

No, I'm not against *al fresco* sex. Looking back, some of my best sessions have been out-of-doors. It is not only a very welcome change of scene that can often make it very good indeed, but there is an added sensuousness which comes from the constant caress, even on a hot day, of pure out-door air circulating round the bodies. But the conditions have got to be right.

We once had a house with a garden surrounded by a high wall, which shielded it completely from the windows of the nearby houses. During the summer we used to spread two Li-Los, which we had had sewn side by side in a large cool white cotton bag, on a travelling rug and stretch out naked on them in the sun.

Every time we did this, we convinced ourselves that our primary object was sunbathing, but unfailingly, sooner or later the heat and the little breeze which always played around in the garden would make one or both of us feel randy. Even when we made contact, we still went on pretending that we were sunbathing by making it as leisurely and lazy a session as possible, relying on finger-tips more than tongue-tips, so that we moved only a little. Even when we felt the need to couple we would lie like that for half-an-hour or more, without movement, just lie there and let the sun and breeze kiss our bodies, and feel the inward flow of sensations moving round belly and thighs, penis and balls, womb and vagina, slowly but inexorably building up of their own accord until the moment came that we could hold back no longer. Just three or four swings of the buttocks were then enough to climax us with huge noisy gasps of out-rushing breath.

I am dead against Carezza, which is a form of intercourse in which the couple lie joined for an hour or more without making any movement, and then part without climaxing—they say, because the tensions have disappeared and there is no need for orgasm. The devotees of this method claim terrific spiritual satisfaction from it, and I can, I think, appreciate what they mean. But it is physically dangerous for the man if practised often, because the prostate becomes congested and if it is not emptied by ejaculation, inflammation will be set up, and over a period the gland will enlarge until eventually surgery becomes necessary.

But the Carezza people do have something. There is this strange and thrilling inward flow of sensations which I have already mentioned, and so long as the session ends in orgasm, no harm is done. It takes quite a lot of practice to keep penis and clitoris erect, and lips swollen, but it can most assuredly be done and the Sensuous Couple would, I am sure, find it a worthwhile technique to develop.

I realise that except in isolated parts of the country, not many people have suitably secure gardens in which they can make love. But most people have a car these days, and it is possible still to find secret secluded spots, though there aren't many left. If you have found such a spot, do provide yourself with portable equipment which is going to make your lovemaking as comfortable as possible.

Our climate is against *al fresco* lovemaking as a frequent pastime, but you may sometimes find yourself in a warm Mediterranean place by the sea, or even north, in the warm Scandinavian summer.

It is sometimes possible to find a deserted spot on the shore, away from the fashionable crowded beaches. If you ever do find yourself in such a situation, try this workout.

Choose a spot where the sand is firm. Soft sand can play havoc in several areas of naked bodies. Spread out your towels and go into your lovemaking. When the time comes to couple, go down to the water's edge.

There the Sensuous Man lies down on his back, his legs in the sea up to his waist. The Sensuous Woman lies on him, and as the waves break gently over them, she takes charge of proceedings and brings about their climaxes. If she can time it so that they have the first throb of orgasm as a wave breaks over them, sensations can be fantastic. I know, because we once had a private beach in a warm country where we could do this.

It may need a good deal of ingenuity to assure security and comfort—but if you can't, give up the idea—but if you can, an occasional out-door session can be a wild experience.

CHAPTER THIRTEEN

STATUS SYMBOLS

For some reason or other, now that we discuss sex more freely and frankly we've just had to introduce status into our lovemaking. Keeping up with the Joneses sexually has become in some quarters a kind of madness and though it may not cost anything financially, it can be emotionally very expensive indeed.

Betty's girl-friend Elsie, who lives next door, tells her that she and her husband Jack make love every day, sometimes twice a day. Betty and her husband George only make it twice a week. Betty, not understanding that Elsie and Jack's needs are different from her own and George's, demands that George shall make love to her more often. George, who likes to please Betty as much as he can, tries to oblige. In a short time he begins to find the effort a bit too much, and in her heart, too, Betty knows that she doesn't need more than two or three orgasms a week. But she is determined to keep up with Elsie and when George points out that it's impossible, the sparks begin to fly. What before was a happy, satisfying relationship begins to go down the hill. That's what I mean by emotional cost.

All this sex-status business started about half a century ago, when Marie Stopes and one or two others reminded women that they could have orgasms like men, and had as much right to find sex as pleasurable as their husbands did.

This was a good thing, but unfortunately it wasn't handled in quite the right way, for the women were told that it was the responsibility of their husbands to bring them to a climax *every* time they made love, and that a man who couldn't do precisely that was no great shakes as a lover. The women passed on the message to their husbands, and since every man wants to be a successful lover, the ability to satisfy their partners every time they made love became a status symbol for men, and a husband who could do this became a status symbol for women.

When neither acquired these status symbols for the reason that some men just don't have the sexual imagination to learn how to climax a woman, or because some women are often quite happy to be pleasured without climaxing every time, conflict once again invaded the love-bed. However, a largish number of couples did acquire the status symbol of "Every Time An Orgasm", and for them, after a time it became old hat, and they had to search for a new status symbol.

This time it was simultaneous orgasm. Unhappily a crowd of so-called sex-experts jumped on this bandwaggon, and cracked it up for all they were worth. As one said, "Simultaneous orgasm is the most perfect of all sexual experiences. When a couple reach their climax at the same moment they can call themselves with every justification, lovers par excellence, because not only are the respective climaxes the most intense they can ever be, at the moment of mutual climax the lovers become truly fused into one being."

Poppycock!

What these same experts did not explain was that the timing of simultaneous orgasm is so tricky that even really expert lovers cannot achieve it at will. When it happens, even for them, more often than not the two orgasms are less intense than the tandem orgasms which truly skilful lovers most often use, in which the woman leads off and the man follows. And why? Two reasons: In trying to climax together the couple are usually concentrating so much on this result that they don't pay the attention they should to the build-up techniques; and, second, if the man happens to climax first, more often than not he can't continue long enough to bring his partner off with his penis and has to get off her and finish with finger or mouth—which necessitates a break in her build-up and could put her right off—while if the man makes sure that his partner comes before he does, while he is bringing himself to the same happy conclusion, he is giving his partner an extra bonus of sensations; because the woman's orgasm-sensations last much longer than the man's.

This coming together remained the status symbol until a few years back when Masters and Johnson introduced Multiple Orgasms. Quite a number of sexually well-attuned women before then had been having the experience of coming off two or three times in fairly quick succession to the man's once during a single session, had enjoyed it, but hadn't written home about it. It didn't always happen, but when it did it was an extra.

Then Masters and Johnson came along and announced that *all women are capable of having multiple orgasms whenever they want to*. So in America multiple orgasms have now become the No. 1 Sex Status Symbol; and there are signs that we are in danger of it becoming so here. In some quarters, especially in the United States, it is not a matter of three or four orgasms in one session, but ten, twenty, thirty in an hour. The other day I read about a woman who can have as many as a hundred in an hour; though what she gets out of it, I can't think, except a sore clitoris and a dull, nagging ache in the small of the back.

For most women, however, multiple orgasm is a technique that has to be acquired, and there are many women around who just can't get the hang of it at all. The truth is, there is no need for them to get the hang of it, for the simple reason that their first orgasm is so good, they are completely satisfied by it.

But I have evidence, too, that, like mutual climaxes, multiple orgasm as a status symbol is causing a great deal of sexual unhappiness. Women who can't climax two or three times are worrying because they think they must have something wrong with them; and men who can't bring their partners off more than once are beginning to lose faith in themselves as lovers. If they go on, they will eventually feel so sexually inadequate, they will *become* completely inadequate and won't be able to make love at all.

The Sensuous Couple, in my book, has absolutely nothing to do with Sex Status Symbols. They don't go in for competitions. They don't care much about other people's love making, except they are sad when they hear that either through lack of imagination, ignorance, carelessness or some other cause, a couple haven't had, or never do have, good sessions.

Status Sex is about as silly a concept that it is possible to come up with. For heaven's sake, let's be natural about our loving, using the talents we have been given to the best of our ability, skills and imagination.

When they embark on a session the Sensuous Couple have three ends in view:

(a) To provide one another with a crescendo of sensuous pleasure:

(b) To have fun doing it:

(c) To climax with the greatest bang possible, not only for the relief from physical tensions, but to show each other how deep their mutual love is. Simultaneous orgasms, multiple orgasms, how often you make it—all are meaningless unless these three conditions are fulfilled, and the Sensuous Couple knows it.

CHAPTER FOURTEEN

WHAT IS IT ABOUT CHAMPAGNE?

It is recorded that after his wedding-night, the young Prince Arthur, brother of Henry VIII, put his head out of the bed-curtains and remarked to his Gentlemen-in-Waiting, "By my troth, gentlemen, this loving is a thirsty business."

Most people would agree with him, and, I think, all Sensuous Couples, who wise as they are, provide themselves with liquid refreshment of some kind or another, strategically placed on the bedside table, before they begin.

I first learned about drinking champagne in bed when I was a young student in Paris some time before the Second World War. I had a very pleasant arrangement with an art student who let me share her studio home in return for my services as a model and a lover, and the vin ordinaire. With no worries about rent or sustenance, I was able to make my allowance go considerably farther than it would otherwise have gone.

She was a year or two older than I was; and at twenty-two or twenty-three was already an accomplished Sensuous Woman. It was she who put me on the road to becoming a Sensuous Man; and I like to think I was such an apt pupil that before very long we could have claimed to be a Sensuous Couple.

There's a great song and dance made about our

young generation being permissive and having no sense of sexual decency, with their swinging and group-sex and public nudity. But, believe me, they are not doing anything that has not been done before.

Julie was popular and she had many friends. Two or three couples from the chorus of the Folies-Bergère lived in other rooms in the tall old Montmartre house, in the shadow of the Sacré Soeur. The studio was up under the eaves, a very large room, and from its windows we had a magnificent view of Paris.

As the studio was the most commodious room in the house, it was the scene most evenings of gatherings of the other inhabitants, and of those from nearby houses, among them other artists and their models, students from the university, and other young people. They brought their own bread, sausage, cheese and wine, and talked about the state of the world and how to put it to rights, just as, I'm told, the young nowadays do.

Up a short flight from the studio landing was a flat roof where Julie and I and the Folies-Bergère dancers sunbathed naked under the Parisian summer sun, on mattresses which we had dragged up there. If the spirit moved us we made love, and if one couple started, this more often than not started the others off, too, so that there were often three or four young Sensuous Couples making love side by side on the mattresses, which were all pushed together to form one great bed.

The wonderful thing about it was that they were all so uninhibited it seemed so right. There was nothing contrived about it; we were responding to love and our instincts. I never heard a salacious comment; but there was a great deal of laughter and fun.

I've been thinking that I might be getting off the point, but on consideration, I don't think I have. Speaking personally, I know that the eighteen months I spent in this glorious company were the making of me sexually. I had gone to Paris privately raring to go, but held back from going by the strict religious background of my home-life. I had come to terms with masturbation after a long argument with myself in which pure adolescent logic had triumphantly freed me from guilt-feelings; but when it came to dipping my wick in the receptacle Nature had provided for its dipping, I could not bring myself to enjoy it because my parents had dinned into me, "Man isn't meant to enjoy sex unless his union is blessed by marriage vows."

At our first encounter, Julie, recognising a kindred sexual appetite, albeit an ethically imprisoned one, had taken me by storm. It was such a fantastic experience for me, that more than forty years later, I can relive every second of it. But the most important outcome for me was that it convinced me that any man or woman endowed with the physical talents to make such experiences possible could not be behaving immorally unless they denied those talents their natural rein, provided they had a happy and willing partner; and the uninhibited sexual enjoyment of our friends convinced me that a bit of paper cannot make any difference to the experience of love-committed sex.

Now the champagne.

Among our friends was a young artist who, despite being a very good painter, was the pampered son of a wealthy industrialist. He never flashed his riches around, but we all knew that he did not have to worry about where the next tube of burnt sienna was coming from.

I was well on the way to becoming Julie's Sensuous Partner—I suppose we had been lovers about three months—when Edouard had his twenty-first birthday. He asked Julie if he could have a small celebration in the studio for his Paris friends who would not be able to go to the official show put on by his parents.

During the afternoon crates of seafood of every description were delivered by Prunier, who at the same time dumped three cases of Veuve Clicquot in our already cluttered living-quarters. To my surprise, Julie pounced first on the champagne. Under her direction I broke open the cases, and together we compelled them into the lead-lined ice-box which Prunier had decided we needed to go with them. All, that is, but two, which she secreted at the back of one of the cupboards in our box-like kitchen, declaiming dramatically, *"Couvre"* (cover-charge, perks).

It was a wild, mad, wonderful, free, uninhibited, earthy, sexy party. After an hour or two not one of us had a stitch of clothing on us—it was a sweltering August night. Before midnight the roof was unable to cope, and the studio, too, became the *mise en scène* of a Fellini orgy, except there was nothing orgiastic about it—just young people, attached to one another at least by strong affection, endowed with the sexual energy to match their love-bound needs.

"It's the champagne!" Julie told me, when I asked her what was happening.

In 1929 at the age of eighteen, I was a stranger to champagne. I just could not believe that the delicious, ice-cold, much superior alternative to the vin ordinaire, could have this liberating effect.

Two days later, however, I was taught a new lesson.

Julie and I were in the habit of devoting most afternoons to one or more sessions of lovemaking, because by the time our friends had left us in the early hours of the morning, we were mostly ready for sleep.

I had had a free morning from the Sorbonne, and had been modelling for Julie yet again. Her painting had gone well, and we were in a good mood when we flopped on the bed after the post-midday sandwich.

It was very warm. It was showery, so that we could not go up to the roof. Though we had opened the studio door and the windows, there was no movement of air. By the end of our first encounter, we were not only satiated, but limp—in more senses than one—and more wet than usual.

After a few minutes of stillness while we recovered our breaths, Julie fetched one of our two bottles of purloined Veuve Clicquot which, without telling me, she had put in the kitchen sink under a running (cold) tap. We had no champagne glasses. (Looking back, I am sure champagne glasses would have been inhibiting because they have such a social gloss.) We drank our champagne from vin ordinaire tumblers.

With the first gulp I felt myself becoming revitalised. After the second, where a moment or two before I would have assured anyone interested and had the courtesy to listen, that my penis had done his bit for the day, I became conscious of him stirring and re-swelling, preparing for further action. I was amazed!

I reached out a hand and exploratorily put it on Julie. To my surprise, she was already swollen and moist.

She smiled at me with that special encouraging smile that never failed to bring me to life when sexual energy seemed to have flagged. Then she dipped her fingers in her tumbler and bathed my penis in the icy champagne. He at once nodded his comprehension and came to attention. Within minutes we were at it again.

You can get eight glasses from a bottle of champagne—four each. By the time the bottle was empty we had had five fantastic grand climaxes!

I am not exaggerating!

As I have grown older, I have, from time to time, when we have embarked on Special Occasion Love-making, taken champagne to bed and we have preferred to drink it there instead of at the dining-table. It has never failed to repeat for me that first experience, and I am quite certain that I am not merely reliving the past.

There *is* something about champagne. I don't know what it is, and I haven't bothered to find out, because I can see no point spending time trying to discover what it is that unfailingly puts lead in the pencil, so long as it continues to happen.

I am equally certain that it does not work only for me and the various partners on whom I have experimented.

So, I recommend it to all Sensuous Couples, who have not made the discovery for themselves, as a now-and-again aid to loving.

Half a bottle between two is equal to at least one-plus-two very desirable orgasms! Cheap at the price!

CHAPTER FIFTEEN

SHARED FANTASIES

I know a young man who, every time he makes love to his wife in a rear-entry position, imagines he is making love with a boy. Yet, he has never had a homophile experience in his life, and is certain he would run a mile if another man attempted to make a pass at him.

It happened quite out of the blue once when they were making love. He could have done nothing to prevent it. But when he climaxed, he had a tremendous orgasm, and now the subconscious memory of this orgasm automatically sparks off his fantasy because deep in his mind he wants to experience its sensations again.

(There is an explanation for this young man's strange fantasy, but I needn't go into it here. It is not so uncommon a fantasy as one might think, nor is the equivalent woman's fantasy.)

We all day-dream from time to time, not just in connection with sex, but in the other compartments of which our lives are made up. There is a little bit of Walter Mitty in all of us. We all have our hopes and our ideals and our standards, and it doesn't do us any harm if now and again we indulge ourselves in a small pretence that we are St George rescuing the damsel, Abraham Lincoln at Gettysburg, a jumbo-jet pilot,

Richard Nixon or Ted Heath.

There is no harm in sexual fantasising, either, though people are inclined to get a bit worked up about it, and imagine themselves to be all kinds of kinky monsters because practically every sex daydream dreamed while you are making love turns you on dramatically and gives you a special quality climax. Whether you know it or not, this is why you are daydreaming. You want something you don't usually get.

There are several kinds of sexual fantasies, and a man or woman may have quite a repertoire of different ones. For example, a man may imagine his partner is Brigitte Bardot one day and that he is Don Juan the next; a woman may imagine her lover is Dr Kildare on Wednesday and that she is Messalina on Sunday. Usually, however, the day-dream is always of the same type.

By the way, the majority of fantasisers don't daydream every time they make love. On the other hand, there are some who are compulsive fantasisers who have to dream up their fantasies *every* time, otherwise there can be no lovemaking at all, because without the particular day-dream there's no arousal of any kind, which, in the case of the man, can mean no erection and all that that signifies.

Such compulsive fantasising is a little bit kinky, but who can say that a man or woman shall be denied the right to sex simply because the only thing that turns them on is a day-dream? Certainly not me!

One thing about sexual fantasies—if they are to be successful they have to be acted out as far as possible. The Sensuous Partner must really take on the form of Richard Burton or Sophia Loren in the imagination if they are to have the desired effect.

This type of fantasy can remain, in fact should remain, a secret from the partner. I cannot imagine any man or woman being made happy by the thought that they are not being loved for themselves alone, but are substitutes for imaginary partners. But apart from the compulsive fantasies, most of which must be shared, e.g. the bondage, master-and-mistress, mistress-and-slave fantasies, since to work at all require the active co-operation of the partner, there are a number of harmless fantasies which the Sensuous Couple can share, purely because they are able to talk to and understand one another.

Shared fantasies are quite a legitimate technique, since they are really just another way of turning one on; and they can also be fun to act out.

There is a couple who have devised an elaborate charade. They pretend they are a married woman and her lover. When the "lover" can get the afternoon off, he telephones his "mistress" and asks if the coast is clear. It invariably is, of course, but very occasionally they pretend it is not—they are that thorough.

On arrival at the house, the "lover" is met at the door by his "mistress" in a specially frilly negligée that she keeps for these occasions. All the way up the garden path, he glances surreptitiously at the neighbours' windows, and if he is seen by one of them, the situation is made much more piquant.

Though they said their farewells only a few hours before, they greet one another as though this was their first meeting for weeks. He asks when the husband is due home, and makes a note of the time he must leave. Great care is taken that he leaves no trace in the sitting-room or bedroom which might give the game away to the husband. They make love with a desperate urgency, and then find they have time for another session. Every so often they look at the clock, and at ten to five precisely he dresses, helps her to make the bed, and gives her a final close embrace. She stands at the top of the stairs naked, and blows him kisses as he lets himself out of the front-door.

She baths, puts on a new face and dresses, and when he returns at five to six, his customary husband-time, she is in the hall waiting for him.

"You look radiant," he says.

"Do I?" she says. "That's because you have come home."

"It wouldn't surprise me if you were having a bit on the side. You generally look like that after we've had a good one."

"How can you suggest such a thing!" she exclaims in mock consternation. "You know I love only you!"

"Prove it," he says.

"Later," she smiles. "Your dinner will spoil if it has to be kept waiting."

Not all fantasy charades are as elaborate as this one, but the nearer the actual scene is to the imaginary one, the greater the effect. Quite a number of women like to fantasise that they are being raped. If the husband is not a Sensuous Man, who understands these things and knows what a special desire can mean to the quality of a session, he can act the fantasy out. Usually it is enough for the Sensuous Woman to be spread-eagled on the bed, her hands and feet lightly bound to the ends of the bed. Many a Sensuous Partner co-operating to this extent has found that he, too, gets a different kick from the usual one.

Then there is the woman who every now and again likes to fantasise that she is a prostitute. Some women can take this quite a long way in the imagination, but if the Sensuous Partner will act out the roles of various clients, actually puts the cash under the pink vase on the table before they start, the illusion is much more real, the effects much more satisfying.

A truly Sensuous Man ought to be able to co-operate in his partner's fantasies in such a way that he gets a special kick out of the role he is asked to play; and the Sensuous Woman should be able to react in the same way to his.

He is a handsome, dashing, fiery Arab sheik, who leaps from his snow-white charger, flings himself into his tent (bedroom), finds his favourite concubine conveniently there, throws her on the divan and takes her before he has thought to take off his *kaffiyeh* and *cambaz*. He is a shy but rampant youth having a go for the first time, who has to be taught what to do by a more experienced partner. The possibilities are innumerable.

The Sensuous Couple playing these games enter completely into the spirit of them. Though seriously played they can, at the same time, be fun.

CHAPTER SIXTEEN

TROILISM, SWINGING, GROUP SEX AND THE SENSUOUS COUPLE

I know that the devotees of these three variations of sexual activities claim that through them their sex lives take on a new lease, and the relationship which was in danger of foundering, is saved from that disaster.

For the would-be Sensuous Couple who have not advanced quite so far as this in sexual sophistication, let me define what the terms mean.

Troilism describes the situation when a couple and a third person make love to one another at the same time. If the third person is a woman, the combination is called German Troilism; if the third person is a man, it is called Japanese Troilism. Whether German or Japanese, it nearly always transpires that the combination can only work if one of the couple is bisexual, i.e. is capable of making love with a member of the same sex as well as with the opposite sex.

There are lots of bisexuals about, more than has been realised up to now. The case for bisexuality—or as I prefer to call it, ambisexuality—can be argued with logic, for when we are in the womb, up to quite a late stage of our uterine development, we have the genitals of both male and female.

Even now as adults, the man produces a certain amount of the female sex hormones, and the woman's sexual drive—her libido—is regulated by the male sex hormone, testosterone, which also regulates the man's sex-drive. In fact, a very good case can be made out for the idea that the ambisexual represents the normal in sex, and the heterosexual and the purely homosexual, the abnormal. But that's another story and doesn't really concern us here, except that I will say that evidence I have collected quite definitely reveals that the ambisexual is an invariably highly Sensuous Person. But do please take note—I am not suggesting that all highly Sensuous Persons are ambisexual.

I'm sorry to have gone off the tracks a little bit

there, but I just had to get it off my chest. What I am really getting at is this—because one of the partners is ambisexual, I can foresee all sorts of complications setting in in both kinds of Troilism, especially the Japanese variety. Even a Sensuous Woman is jealous of her partner's activities, and I know of several cases in which the homophile activities of the two males have been as upsetting for the woman as if the other partner had been another woman.

I have to concede, though, that most Sensuous Men —who, in any case, are much more voyeurs than women; that is to say, are more turned on than women are by watching a couple making love—are turned on by watching two women together. (The Danes exploit this somewhat strange quirk, by beginning all their "live" sex-shows with a lesbian act.) In German Troilism, therefore, the man is less likely to be affected by his Sensuous Partner's involvement with a third person. On the other hand, however, if he tries out his chances with the odd girl out, he is more than likely to have trouble with his Sensuous Partner.

Swinging is mate-swapping. There are two forms of it.

(a) Two couples join forces and swap partners, going off into separate bedrooms to have intercourse:

(b) A number of couples meet, the men put a personal belonging, usually their car-keys, into a pool, the women choose from the objects in the pool, pair off with the man to whom it belongs, and retreats to some private spot to make love with him.

I can see danger in this, too. Supposing the fly-by-night partner is a vastly superior lover compared with the permanent partner? Is the sex-life of the couple ever going to be the same again? I doubt it.

Some swingers do get a kick out of it; not out of the actual experiences, but out of recounting their experiences to one another while they are having a session themselves. It seems to me, however, that this is a brand of kinkiness that can lead to all sorts of trouble. Supposing one or both crack up the experience so much that they realise that whatever they may do together they won't be able to repeat the experience with one another? Their eagerness to boast then has exactly the opposite effect they wanted it to have. They will lose confidence in their partner's sexual abilities and in their own.

Group sex is the meeting together of eight or a dozen or more couples who make love together in the same room in full view of one another. (It is the modern equivalent of the pagan orgy, except that the party doesn't get drunk and out of hand.) By the rules of the game, you can couple up with anyone present who is prepared to accept you as a partner, or you can stick with your own partner.

To my way of thinking, of the three varieties, this is the least dangerous. Even if a couple decide to switch, because the whole session takes place in full view of all, it is possible for the partners to keep an eye on each other, which greatly reduces the risk of jealousy rearing its ugly head.

In my book, the truly Sensuous Couple will shy away from troilism and swinging. The definition of a Sensuous Couple not only presupposes the combination of a Sensuous Man and a Sensuous Woman, but such a combination of male and female sensuousness that they have no need of outside help of any kind to enable them to express their love for one another in physical terms that are deeply and completely satisfying.

Group sex is a rather different kettle of fish. But here again I can only see it being free of risk, if the Sensuous Couple keep to themselves. We are all voyeurs to a rather greater degree than we realise, and seeing others making love can be fascinatingly stimulating. Not only that, by watching others at it, one can nearly always pick up tips that will help even the most imaginative of us to inject some new ideas into our private sessions; and that is always very worthwhile.

But even group sex should not be a must in the life of a truly Sensuous Couple. If the opportunity arises, and both Sensuous Partners think the experience might be useful, O.K. But I think that if the Couple can justifiably claim to be Sensuous, they should be able to get along very well without this sort of help.

What I am really getting at is this! The combined sexual imaginations of the Sensuous Couple should be quite capable of keeping them sexually happy indefinitely. Only such couples who have this degree of imagination and the skills which automatically accompany it can rank themselves as really sensuous.

CHAPTER SEVENTEEN

ARE SEX AIDS ALLOWED?

Of course they are!

Anything that helps to increase the lovemaking experience is permissible. If this were not so, the dictum that the aim of each session should be that the partners should show their love for one another by providing each other with the most intense build-up of sensations and the most obliterating of climaxes would not hold water.

There will, of course, be Sensuous Couples whose techniques are so well-developed that their natural endowments do not need any artificial aids to help them produce the desired results. On the other hand, quite a number of really highly developed Sensuous Couples are not too proud to admit that this or that aid can heighten their experience.

There are, for example, clitoral stimulators of various types, which the man fixes over his penis in such a position that when he puts his penis in the vagina, a little knob on the appliance makes direct contact with the clitoral area and stimulates it directly as he swings or thrusts. Then there is the rubber ring studded with little flexible tongues of rubber, which the man slips on to his penis just below the rim. When he puts his penis into the vagina, the ring goes in with it, and as he moves his penis backwards and forwards, the little tongues of rubber stimulate the walls of the vagina, and apparently gives the woman a new experience.

There are so-called "contoured" sheaths, too, which have the same aim. They have raised designs on them which stimulate the vaginals walls. I don't think they will appeal to the Sensuous Man, because, though they may do something for his Sensuous Partner, they are a dead loss to him.

The manufacturers have not yet discovered a way of contouring thin sheaths, and their present product is of very heavy latex indeed. This has the effect of completely deadening all sensations in the penis, both in and out of the vagina.

I suppose no sensible Sensuous Couple these days is without a personal operated vibrator. This vibrator is shaped something like a penis, and it is mostly used for clitoral stimulation, being much less tiring than manual stimulation. There must be occasions when even a Sensuous Couple want to take short cuts.

However, I agree with "J", who in *The Sensuous Woman*, suggested that the use of a vibrator was the surest way of teaching a woman to have multiple orgasms. If a Sensuous Woman who doesn't yet have multiple orgasms wants to join that particular sex rat-race, she will get a great deal of help from her personal vibrator.

As I said earlier, anything that helps to heighten the love-experience is valid; anything, that is, in the way of appliances. The Sensuous Couple knows, without my telling them, that they should not be taken in by the claims of this or that potion or food "to restore sexual vitality and assure virility." There is nothing in the world that will do that, and to be tempted into buying such things is merely answering an invitation to throw your money away.

CHAPTER EIGHTEEN

IN THE AFTERGLOW

No matter in what position the Sensuous Couple connect for the Grand Finale, after they have both climaxed they do not separate until the penis has shrunk and slipped out of the vagina of its own accord.

By the time this has happened, they will have come back to earth again. They will exchange gentle kisses of the lips, cheeks and eyelids; they will whisper to one another how fantastically good it was, and say their mutual "Thank yous".

As soon as he disconnects, the Sensuous Man dries off his Sensuous Partner's sex-lips and the ridge below them, and his penis with the Kleenex he has beside his bed for this purpose. Then he pulls up the bed covers and puts out the light.

They snuggle down in one another's arms, and with a final kiss close their eyes for sleep.

Their last thought?

"That was so good. We must do it again sometime —very soon!"

They deserve their luck. They've taken the trouble to turn themselves into a Sensuous Couple, and can at last really claim to be Sensuous Man and Sensuous Woman.

NEL BESTSELLERS

Crime

W002 773	THE LIGHT OF DAY	Eric Ambler	25p
W002 786	ABILITY TO KILL	Eric Ambler	25p
W002 799	THE MURDER LEAGUE	Robert L. Fish	30p
W002 876	MURDER MUST ADVERTISE	Dorothy L. Sayers	35p
W002 849	STRONG POISON	Dorothy L. Sayers	30p
W002 848	CLOUDS OF WITNESS	Dorothy L. Sayers	35p
W002 845	THE DOCUMENTS IN THE CASE	Dorothy L. Sayers	30p
W002 877	WHOSE BODY?	Dorothy L. Sayers	30p
W002 749	THE NINE TAILORS	Dorothy L. Sayers	30p
W002 871	THE UNPLEASANTNESS AT THE BELLONA CLUB	Dorothy L. Sayers	30p
W002 750	FIVE RED HERRINGS	Dorothy L. Sayers	30p
W002 826	UNNATURAL DEATH	Dorothy L. Sayers	30p
W003 011	GAUDY NIGHT	Dorothy L. Sayers	40p
W002 870	BLOODY MAMA	Robert Thom	25p

Fiction

W002 755	PAID SERVANT	E. R. Braithwaite	30p
T005 801	RIFIFI IN NEW YORK	Auguste le Breton	30p
W002 743	HARRISON HIGH	John Farris	40p
W002 861	THE GIRL FROM HARRISON HIGH	John Farris	40p
W002 833	THE CRAZY LADIES	Joyce Elbert	40p
T007 030	A TIME OF PREDATORS	Joe Gores	30p
W002 424	CHILDREN OF KAYWANA	Edgar Mittelholzer	37½p
W002 425	KAYWANA STOCK	Edgar Mittelholzer	37½p
W002 426	KAYWANA BLOOD	Edgar Mittelholzer	37½p
T009 084	SIR, YOU BASTARD	G. F. Newman	40p
W002 881	THE FORTUNATE PILGRIM	Mario Puzo	35p
W002 752	THE HARRAD EXPERIMENT	Robert H. Rimmer	30p
W002 920	PROPOSITION 31	Robert H. Rimmer	30p
W002 427	THE ZOLOTOV AFFAIR	Robert H. Rimmer	25p
W002 704	THE REBELLION OF YALE MARRATT	Robert H. Rimmer	30p
W002 896	THE CARPETBAGGERS	Harold Robbins	75p
W002 918	THE ADVENTURERS	Harold Robbins	75p
W002 941	A STONE FOR DANNY FISHER	Harold Robbins	50p
W002 654	NEVER LOVE A STRANGER	Harold Robbins	60p
W002 653	THE DREAM MERCHANTS	Harold Robbins	60p
W002 917	WHERE LOVE HAS GONE	Harold Robbins	60p
W002 155	NEVER LEAVE ME	Harold Robbins	25p
T006 743	THE INHERITORS	Harold Robbins	60p
T009 467	STILETTO	Harold Robbins	30p
W002 761	THE SEVEN MINUTES	Irving Wallace	75p
W002 580	THE BEAUTIFUL COUPLE	William Woolfolk	37½p
W002 312	BRIDE OF LIBERTY	Frank Yerby	25p
W002 479	AN ODOUR OF SANCTITY	Frank Yerby	50p
W002 916	BENTON'S ROW	Frank Yerby	40p
W002 822	GILLIAN	Frank Yerby	40p
W002 895	CAPTAIN REBEL	Frank Yerby	30p
W002 010	THE VIXENS	Frank Yerby	40p
W003 007	A WOMAN CALLED FANCY	Frank Yerby	30p
W002 223	THE OLD GODS LAUGH	Frank Yerby	25p

Science Fiction

T009 696	GLORY ROAD	Robert Heinlein	40p
W002 844	STRANGER IN A STRANGE LAND	Robert Heinlein	60p
W002 630	THE MAN WHO SOLD THE MOON	Robert Heinlein	30p
W002 386	PODKAYNE OF MARS	Robert Heinlein	30p
W002 449	THE MOON IS A HARSH MISTRESS	Robert Heinlein	40p
W002 754	DUNE	Frank Herbert	60p
W002 911	SANTAROGA BARRIER	Frank Herbert	30p
W002 641	NIGHT WALK	Bob Shaw	25p
W002 716	SHADOW OF HEAVEN	Bob Shaw	25p

NEL BESTSELLERS

NEL, P.O. BOX 11, FALMOUTH, CORNWALL

Please send cheque or postal order. Allow 4p per book to cover postage and packing (Overseas 5p per book).

Name..

Address ....

....

Title ....

(JUNE)